# SOUTHERN PACIFIC
# DAYLIGHT
# STEAM LOCOMOTIVES

## KENNETH G. JOHNSEN

**specialtypress**
PUBLISHERS AND WHOLESALERS

Published by
Specialty Press Publishers and Wholesalers
39966 Grand Avenue
North Branch, MN 55056
United States of America
(800) 895-4585 or (651) 277-1400
www.specialtypress.com

Distributed in the UK and Europe by
Midland Publishing
4 Watling Drive
Hinckley LE10 3EY, England
Tel: 01455 254 450 Fax: 01455 233 737
www.midlandcountiessuperstore.com

ISBN-13  978-1-58007-098-0
ISBN-10  1-58007-098-1

*Front cover:* Southern Pacific GS-4 Daylight locomotive number 4455 steams away at Taylor Yard in Los Angeles on January 8, 1955, just one day after the Coast Daylight made its last steam powered trip. This locomotive would go on to serve until the very end of steam on Southern Pacific, losing its colorful skirting and making the last unscheduled run of a Daylight locomotive in 1958. The GS-4 Class was considered the high point of Daylight design. (Stan Kistler photo from the collection of Tom Gildersleeve)

*Title Page:* Southern Pacific 4451 departs Third & Townsend Station in San Francisco on July 23, 1953. (Jack Pfeifer photo from the collection of Tom Gildersleeve)

*Back cover, top:* Future celebrity 4449 backs down the lead to Los Angeles Union Passenger Terminal in January 1948. This famous Daylight has been seen by more Americans than any other steam locomotive. (Jack Woods photo from the collection of Tom Gildersleeve)

*Back cover, middle:* Southern Pacific's heavy involvement in World War II was due in part to its location on America's West Coast. Many wartime ads were run, including this one admonishing us to "Invest in War Bonds." (Richard Lohse collection)

*Back cover, bottom:* Engineer Doyle McCormack tends the feedwater heater at Sarasota, Florida, on December 7, 1976. (Bob Clark photo)

# TABLE OF CONTENTS

# ABOUT THE AUTHOR

Dr. Ken Johnsen maintains a busy dental practice in Kent, Washington. His interest in trains is among the earliest of his recollections and he began photographing them in 1955 at the age of nine. His first 10 years of life coincided with the final 10 years of steam operation on the Southern Pacific in Johnsen's native California, where he developed a lifelong interest in the Daylights.

The Johnsen family began moving about to various parts of the United States in 1956, finally settling in Washington State in 1965. Dr. Johnsen attended dental school at the University of Washington where he met his wife Lauri, a physical therapist. Ken and Lauri have two sons, Stephen and Gregory.

In the early 1970s Dr. Johnsen was instrumental in returning vintage trolleys to the City of Yakima, Washington, and he is credited with saving the historic Yakima Valley Transportation Company interurban line. He still motors trolleys in Yakima on some summer weekends.

Dr. Johnsen purchased and completely restored a 1913-built Northern Pacific caboose, which is on display in his backyard. Over the years he has written scores of magazine articles and four previous books on railroad subjects, including *Washington Steam Locomotives, Apple Country Interurban, Daylight: 4449's Family Album, and Pacific: 2472's Family Album.*

Photography has been Dr. Johnsen's passion for over 50 years and his work has won numerous awards. With his son Stephen he collects vintage automobiles and electric vehicles and with his son Gregory he builds model trains and a backyard railroad.

Ken and Lauri have backpacked hundreds of miles in the mountains of Western Washington and Montana.

# ACKNOWLEDGMENTS

Telling the Daylight story is a labor of love. I've been in love with these engines since the late 1940s when, as a kid, I drove my tricycle around our yard in Modesto, California, pretending I was the engineer of the Daylight, grimly determined to make sure every start and stop was so smooth that they would be imperceptible to my imaginary passengers. The second photograph I ever took was a slow exposure of a GS-3 in the roundhouse in Los Angeles in 1955 when I was nine years old. Over the years I've come to know a lot of other people who cherish Southern Pacific's Daylights as much as I do.

And I'm still meeting them! Just last year I became acquainted with Richard Lohse who, by virtue of being a few years older than me, had even more chances to savor the Daylights when they were still around. Many thanks go to Richard for providing information, the use of photos, S.P. drawings and advertisements, as well as his recollection of the last unscheduled S.P. Daylight movement under steam.

In 1984 I wrote my first book on the Daylights, *Daylight: 4449's Family Album*. The book in your hands is all new, but contains contributions from some of the people (sadly, many have passed away since 1984) who helped with the original book. Doyle McCormack and I have been friends since 1975 when I was a volunteer on the restoration of the 4449 in Portland. Doyle has never hesitated to share Daylight information with me and his two fascinating contributions to this book are very much appreciated.

The late Jim Boynton was the quintessential steam engineer and a darned good writer too! The paean he penned for me on the Western Pacific versions of the Daylight enriches this book. The late Gerald M. Best and I became friends as a result of the first book and from him I learned one of my favorite behind-the-scenes stories about the Daylight with the sunset emblem on its tender.

Former S.P. fireman Robert McNeel and I began a friendship after the publication of the first book that lasted many years until he passed away a few years ago. In anticipation of the present book, Bob generously lent me his entire photographic collection and penned some recollections. The results speak for themselves.

Many other photographers, collectors, and aficionados (some still with us, some not) have helped in one way or another and I would like to express my thanks to all of them, including Jeff Ainsworth, Allen County Historical Society, Al Augenstein, William Bassler, Leon Callaway, Bob Clark, Guy Denechaud, Guy L. Dunscomb, Dave Edwards, Herman Friedrich, Tom Gildersleeve, Walt Grande, Art Hamilton, Jim Harrison, John Hogan, Don Jardine, Fred Johnsen, Tom King, Stan Kistler, George Lavacot, Arnold Menke, Alan Miller, William G. Moore, Tom Moungovan, Iris Myers, Jim Orem, Terry Parker, Steve Peery, Jack Pfeifer, Tim Repp, Doug Richter, Allen Rider, Roy E. Shepherd, Robert Slocum, Southern Pacific Transportation Company, Fred

*The author living out a dream: at the throttle of a hard-working Daylight GS-4. Photographed on the American Freedom Train in the Blue Mountains of eastern Oregon on October 25, 1975. (Ed Berntsen photo)*

Spurrell, Fred Stindt, Joe R. Thompson, Lee Thwaits, Eugene Vicknair, Harold K. Vollrath, Wilbur Whittaker, Jack Woods, and Ted Wurm. If I have left anyone out, you have my sincerest apology!

It takes a publisher willing to take a risk on a manuscript, and my thanks go to Josh Brown and Steve Hendrickson of Specialty Press for making a reality out of this book.

If my Dad, the late Carl Johnsen, had not taken me to the S.P. yards and roundhouses on "Boys' Days" when I was a kid, I would not have had as much opportunity to learn about and fall in love with the Daylights. I am forever grateful to him for those fun times.

And finally, thanks go to my youngest son Gregory for putting up with my endless questions on how to make the #%@*! computer do what is needed to prepare a manuscript and photos for production. Gregory's expertise with the computer surpasses all belief.

# DEDICATION

To my son Gregory William Johnsen
this book is lovingly dedicated

# INTRODUCTION

Streamliners came of age in the decade of the 1930s. Whether pulled by steam locomotives shrouded in sheet metal or as part of stainless steel diesel-powered articulated trains, streamliners caught the fancy of a country emerging from its worst economic depression.

Sophistication in design progressed from some early laughable attempts by back-shop forces to cover up ancient passenger equipment with shrouding, to carefully planned new trains designed by some of the country's top industrial designers. Their goal was to meld form with function to create an aesthetically pleasing train that was at the same time easy to service and able to perform its duties.

The New York Central Hudsons, the Pennsylvania T1s, the Milwaukee Hiawathas, and many other streamlined steam trains achieved their rightful place in the American consciousness. But it is safe to say none have stirred the souls of so many people or been remembered as fondly as Southern Pacific's great Daylights.

When the first Daylights appeared in 1937, they were immediately bestowed the title of "the most beautiful trains in the world." They were huge, powerful engines that had a perfect blend of form and function. Their dazzling colors caught everyone's eye and their smooth, graceful lines were a pleasure to behold.

From the first beautiful GS-2 Class that launched the Daylight train, the design matured to stronger and even more pleasing proportions, if that is possible. The GS-4 and GS-5 were the high point in design, both aesthetically and in performance. No single diesel unit that succeeded them could ever outperform them or eclipse their good looks.

Progress has not been kind to the streamliners. Look at what Amtrak runs today. Over the years all of the Hudsons, T1s, Hiawathas, and their brethren have disappeared and live now only in our memories and faded photographs. But fate was kind with the Daylights. Through the generosity of the Southern Pacific Company two of them were saved and one of them is in first-class operating condition today.

This book is the story of the Daylights and the story of the lone operating survivor, GS-4 4449. This book contains technical details of Daylight design and operation as well as their operational history, including the 4449's latter day exploits. The aesthetic qualities that made the Daylights stand out are documented in words and stirring photographs. One cannot help but look at the photos and agree that, yes, they definitely were "the most beautiful trains in the world."

Kenneth G. Johnsen
April 2006

---

**CHAPTER ONE**

# DAYLIGHT DESIGN AND DEVELOPMENT

*The age of travel by train is epitomized in this photo at Glendale, California, in 1947. A helpful porter tends to the young lady's needs as the mighty GS-5 patiently waits to get the Coast Daylight underway to San Francisco. In the days before interstate highways, the Southern Pacific offered a swift, safe, scenic trip up the coast to the City by the Bay. (Robert B. McNeel photo)*

For a person born after the middle of the twentieth century, it may be hard to imagine a world in which travel by train was *the* way people got from place to place. For that person the thought of a railroad lavishing fortunes on passenger carrying trains may seem almost comical, or at best an unwise decision.

But the world in the first half of the twentieth century had not known interstate highways and the travel freedom that came with them. Automobiles, while increasingly numerous, were not the comfortable, reliable machines of today. Appurtenances like tool kits and spare tires were carried in cars for a reason: they were frequently needed.

Before the 1950s, generations of people were still alive who had not grown up with the automobile. They saw no need to learn to drive new-fangled horseless carriages when a modest expenditure for a train ticket or trolley token could get them comfortably and effortlessly to their destination.

My grandmother was one such person who never learned to drive. Why should she when she could walk two blocks to the train station in her home town of Reedley, California, board a local train to Fresno, and transfer to the classy San Joaquin Daylight for a swift and comfortable ride to Glendale to pay a visit to her daughter and family? She could dine on the train, have her every need taken care of by a friendly porter, and relax, secure in the knowledge that this big, roomy, and

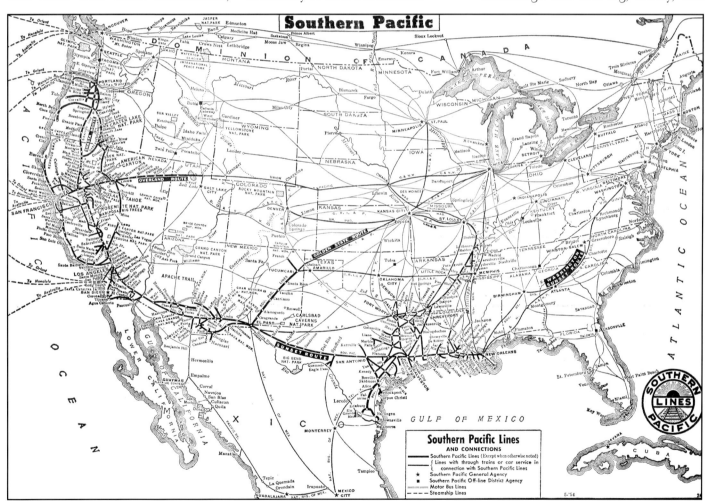

In the Golden Years of steam passenger service, Southern Pacific's empire stretched from Portland, Oregon, to New Orleans, Louisiana, to Ogden, Utah. While the Daylight locomotives spent most of their careers in California on the Coast and San Joaquin routes, they could be seen at one time or another on nearly every section of the far-flung railroad. (Kenneth G. Johnsen collection)

powerful conveyance could be relied on to get her to her destination without problems.

Millions like her across the country took train travel for granted. It was the norm. And for the railroads like Southern Pacific, providing that service in those halcyon days was still seen as a solemn duty.

## Sunset Red and Orange Replace Pearl Gray

The story of the Daylights began on Southern Pacific's Coast Line between Los Angeles and San Francisco. Put into service near the very beginning of the twentieth century, the Coast Line connected the two largest cities in California and within a short time became quite busy.

The railroad experimented with different schedules and slowly evolved the first attempt at a high speed through train, the Daylight Limited of 1922. It carried the numbers 71 and 72 and was neither a daily, nor even a year-round train at first. It lived up to its "Limited" name by making the entire Los Angeles to San Francisco run without stopping to board or detrain passengers. Two service stops along the way were allowed.

The schedule for the Daylight Limited was gradually tightened in increments from 13 to 12 hours, and finally just over 11 hours, start to finish. Popularity of the new train brought about more scheduled runs until it became a year-round daily speedster.

Southern Pacific began supplementing the original coach train with parlor cars and amenities for the pleasure of businessmen traveling between the two metropolises. The 2400 series 4-6-2 Pacific locomotives originally in charge of 71 and 72 were unable to single-handedly keep up with the load. Helpers were required and operating costs went up.

The next level in the progression of motive power evolution was the 4300 series 4-8-2 Mountain type locomotives,

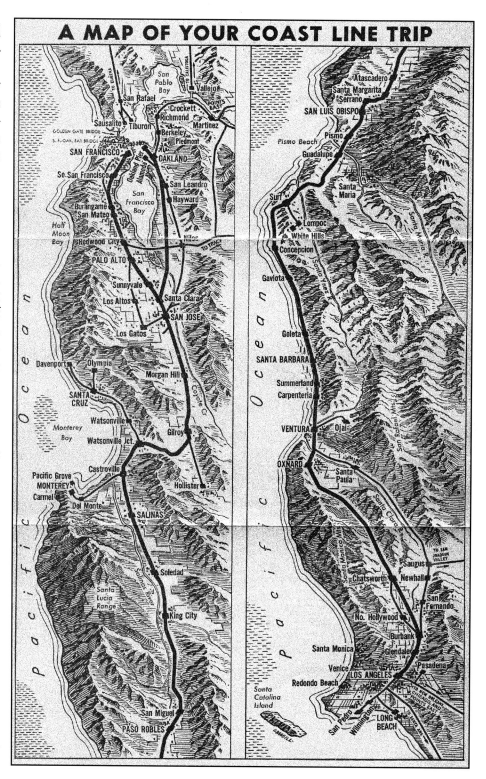

A map of Southern Pacific's Coast Route was included in the souvenir brochure given to each Daylight passenger. A description of the towns and surrounding countryside accompanied the map so that the traveler could stay well informed. (Kenneth G. Johnsen collection)

developed to a fine art by the Southern Pacific in their own shops in Sacramento in the late 1920s. These engines fired easily, started trains easily, and handled well, earning them a special place in the hearts of S.P. enginemen.

*Southern Pacific's 4-6-2 Pacific type locomotives were in charge of long-haul passenger trains on the railroad for many years until the size and weight of trains necessitated larger locomotives. P-10 Class locomotive 2479 is shown at San Luis Obispo in a fine photo taken by Tom Taber on June 26, 1927. In spite of demotions, the 2479 did survive and was placed on display at the Santa Clara County Fairgrounds in San Jose at the end of the steam era. (Arnold S. Menke collection)*

But the march was on to even more power and higher speeds. The 4400 series 4-8-4 Northern type at last became the choice for heavyweight passenger trains, and Baldwin built 14 of them for the Southern Pacific in 1930. The greater size of the firebox on the new 4-8-4s, which necessitated the two-axle trailer truck, allowed a greater heating surface, consequently raising boiler pressure, and increasing power.

It took a couple years for the Great Depression of 1929 to impact the Southern Pacific, but when it finally did, the first reaction was to cut back on the number of passenger trains running up and down the Coast Line, and to relax the schedule of the Daylight.

*The demand for greater power led to the 4-8-2 Mountain type locomotive. Southern Pacific worked on the development of these handsome machines and actually built a number of them in their own shops at Sacramento. Enginemen praised the MT Class for their easy firing characteristics. (Southern Pacific Company photo)*

The 4-8-4 Northern type locomotive was finally settled on for long-haul, heavy passenger trains. Its larger firebox, supported by a two-axle trailer truck, provided greater heating surface and hence greater power. (Southern Pacific Company photo)

Enter Angus D. McDonald as S.P. president in 1933. McDonald was a visionary and a passenger train man. He proposed launching a new Daylight on the Coast Route that would be the finest, most beautiful train in the world. He believed that capitalistic enterprise was what made the nation's economy move, and that large corporations such as the Southern Pacific had a duty to move forward with new enterprises to end the Depression.

Although the country's mobilization in World War II was the primary force that ended the Depression, McDonald's ideas proved to be basically correct. His leadership (and bravery) in launching the new million-dollar Daylight stirred the hearts of most S.P. management, while scaring a few penny pinchers.

The train McDonald proposed for the Daylight was to be all streamlined from end to end. It was to be lightweight and comfortable with air conditioning. It was to be colorful and provide amenities such as meals, which would attract passengers to ride. And it was to be speedy and therefore be pulled by a modern powerful steam engine.

This last requirement reflected McDonald's conservative approach to a radical new train. While his competitors were fiddling with diesels, articulated

Southern Pacific conducted many tests with their steam locomotives to improve economy of operation and safety. GS-1 #4401 is seen at Santa Barbara in 1947 during a test of fusible drop plugs. (Robert B. McNeel photo)

Zephyrs, and the like, McDonald put his trust in the power and reliability of steam locomotives such as those that had been evolving on his railroad.

The unstreamlined GS-1 4-8-4s built by Baldwin were the standard from which the new locomotive design for the Daylights evolved. Ongoing tests by the railroad helped point the

way to a design that was both powerful and speedy. Baldwin, however, would have to bid against upstart Lima Locomotive Works in Lima, Ohio, for the contract to build the new streamlined locomotives for the Daylight.

## Baldwin Upstaged by "Super Power"

"Super Power" was the catchy name given to the larger locomotives built by the Lima Locomotive Works after 1925. It represented an almost fundamentally different concept in steam locomotive design from what had previously been employed at Lima.

"Super Power" locomotives offered greater pulling power along with increased speed. Lima designers and engineers utilized numerous features to realize that goal. Larger capacity boilers with bigger fireboxes were a necessary ingredient. In turn, these advancements required better distribution of locomotive weight over the axles.

Four-wheel trailer trucks had solved the heavier firebox problem. Booster engines were built into the four-wheel trailer trucks, which provided additional tractive effort for starting the locomotive. The booster engines also helped make smoother starts.

*Sandwiched between tracks of the Baltimore and Ohio and the Nickel Plate Road, the Lima Locomotive Works of Lima, Ohio, was the birthplace of "Super Power" locomotives. All of the Daylight locomotives were built at this huge industrial complex. (Allen County Historical Society collection)*

Feedwater heaters and Type E Superheaters preheated the boiler water and helped the steaming characteristics of "Super Power" locomotives. New stronger, lighter steel alloys allowed the construction of boilers capable of higher operating pressures. Increased boiler pressure translated into increased drawbar horsepower, necessary for the higher speeds and pulling power of Lima's new generation of steam locomotives. Cast frames and other refinements at Lima gave "Super Power" a competitive edge over the other builders.

Lima underbid Baldwin for construction of Southern Pacific's GS-2 Class and won the contract. This first class of streamlined Daylight locomotives was mostly the product of Angus McDonald's designers at S.P., but Lima's ingenuity and design skills impressed the railroad enough that subsequent classes showed more and more of the "Super Power" characteristics, reaching their climax in the GS-4 and roller bearing-equipped GS-5 Classes.

The single-headlight, open cab GS-2 Class had an operating boiler pressure of 250 psi. For the similar appearing GS-3 Class, the boiler pressure was pushed up to 280 psi. Diameter of the drivers on the GS-3s also was increased from 73 inches to 80 inches. The GS-4 Class and the GS-5 Class, with their closed cabs and Mars light plus headlight, had 80-inch drivers too. Not only did the larger driver size aid in increasing the speed of the locomotive, but also the consequent lengthening of the wheelbase (and frame) allowed a larger combustion chamber between the firebox and boiler, creating a more efficient heating area.

Fuel Oil Temperature Gauge

Boiler Steam Gauge

Steam Heat Gauge

Feedwater Pump Gauge

Tank Water Level Indicator

Booster Steam Gauge

Signal Foam-meter

Boiler Steam Gauge

Air Brake Gauge

Quadruplex Air Gauge

Locomotive Valve-Pilot

*View of the backhead of a GS-2 Daylight with various appliances pointed out. (Southern Pacific Company collection)*

*Builder's photo of Southern Pacific GS-3 number 4416. The GS-3 models looked like their GS-2 sisters, except they had 80-inch drivers. (Allen County Historical Society collection)*

*Famous face: Southern Pacific GS-4 Daylight face is probably the most recognizable of Lima's creations. The brand new 4454 represents a high point in streamlined steam. (Allen County Historical Society collection)*

Nickel steel alloys used in the boilers of GS-3 and later classes allowed increased boiler pressure, resulting in greater horsepower. Both the GS-4 and GS-5 Classes had an operating pressure of 300 psi and were the most powerful of the Daylights.

The Warbaby GS-6 Class fell back to many pre-GS-3 characteristics owing to the fact that shortages during World War II dictated the use of carbon steel in their boiler construction. Working boiler pressure on the non-glamorous GS-6s was cut back to 260 psi.

Many of the appliances and appurtenances on the Daylights were what are called "vendor items." Examples include Alco Power Reverse, Worthington Feedwater Heater, Pyle-National turbogenerators, Westinghouse Air Pumps, etc. These items were interchangeable with their counterparts on other modern steam locomotives of the 1930s and 1940s.

In blending streamlining with locomotive machinery, Lima designers kept a constant eye toward keeping the

*GS-4 firebox view taken at the factory on March 5, 1942. (Allen County Historical Society collection)*

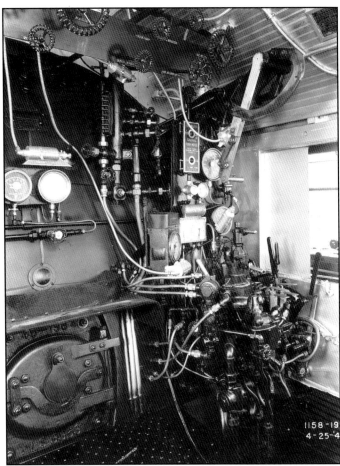

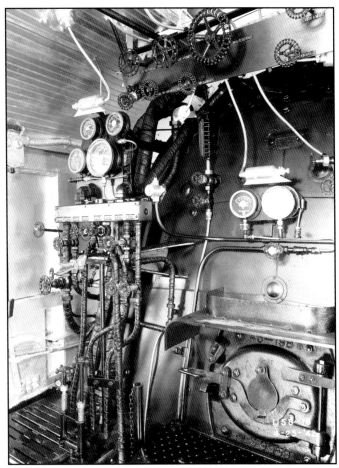

Engineer's side of the cab of a GS-4 from the second group, taken on April 25, 1942. Compare this view to the views of the 4449's cab in Chapter 2. (Allen County Historical Society collection)

View of the fireman's side of the cab of a second group GS-4, taken on April 25, 1942. Lima's inventive photographer, Don Jardine, created a special bank of flood lamps to fully illuminate the interiors of the cabs he photographed. (Allen County Historical Society collection)

Lima's broadside photo of Daylight locomotive number 4454. The 4454 represented the second group of GS-4s, numbers 4450 through 4457. (Allen County Historical Society collection)

Daylight number 4454 was the official photographic representative of the second group of GS-4s. The GS-5s were built along with this group and are indistinguishable from the GS-4s except for their roller bearing journals. (Allen County Historical Society collection)

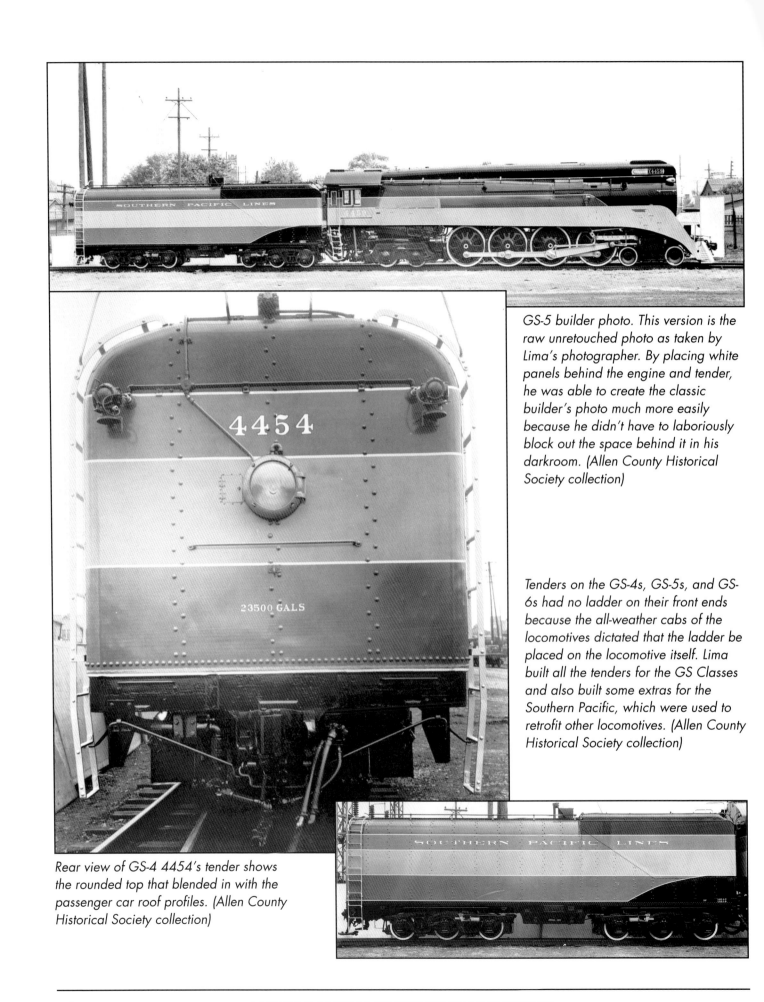

GS-5 builder photo. This version is the raw unretouched photo as taken by Lima's photographer. By placing white panels behind the engine and tender, he was able to create the classic builder's photo much more easily because he didn't have to laboriously block out the space behind it in his darkroom. (Allen County Historical Society collection)

Tenders on the GS-4s, GS-5s, and GS-6s had no ladder on their front ends because the all-weather cabs of the locomotives dictated that the ladder be placed on the locomotive itself. Lima built all the tenders for the GS Classes and also built some extras for the Southern Pacific, which were used to retrofit other locomotives. (Allen County Historical Society collection)

Rear view of GS-4 4454's tender shows the rounded top that blended in with the passenger car roof profiles. (Allen County Historical Society collection)

Type 14600 standard streamline headlight case

Designed for application to streamline type motive power units. Cast aluminum alloy case, sealed for maximum protection to reflector and interior. Reflector edge—mounted in spring clips. Designed for convenient front re-lamping and alignment.

Pyle-National specially designed the headlight casing used on the Daylights for streamlined locomotives. (Fred Spurrell collection)

February 1937
**Southern Pacific Bulletin**

The Southern Pacific Bulletin of February 1937 heralded the "Dawn of a New Daylight." The company was justifiably proud of its new streamliners and

One of the most famous faces in railroading is an S.P. Daylight. GS-5 4459 looks identical to the GS-4 Class, but the journals are all roller bearing. (Allen County Historical Society collection)

servicing of the locomotives as easy as possible. Access hatches were built into the streamlined side skirting to allow servicing of the air pumps, lubricators, etc.

Instead of hiding under the shrouds as on many other streamlined steam engines of the era, components were designed so that they became a functional part of the Daylight's streamlining. For example, the classification lamps were placed in their usual location at the front of the smokebox, but they were made bullet-shaped and silver in color.

The hinged doors of the smokebox front were themselves shaped as part of the streamlining rather than being covered with some inverted bathtub-shaped shroud like the streamliners of other railroads. The Pyle-National headlight was actually designed by Pyle-National to fit into the streamlining as an integral part.

The front bumper beam of the cast engine frame was curved convexly so that it could support a one-piece solid steel pilot whose graceful lines began

spoke of them in glowing terms in the employee magazine. (Kenneth G. Johnsen collection)

the streamlined sweep of the skirting. With the tasteful red, orange, black, and silver paint scheme applied to these engines, they would soon become touted as "the most beautiful in the world."

Southern Pacific's employee Bulletin of February 1937 broke the exciting news of the new locomotives and train.

*Daylight 4436's builder's photo was colorized by Lima because the locomotives were so colorful. (Kenneth G. Johnsen collection)*

The man who created the beautiful and functional photographic record of the Daylights' construction days at Lima was the company's staff photographer, Don Jardine. Jardine was not only an accomplished professional photographer, but he was also something of an inventor, finding creative ways to light his subjects, get the shots under difficult situations, and simplify his follow-up work in the darkroom.

An example of the latter is the large white panels he had set up behind the locomotive to be photographed. They were angled to catch the sun's light and reflect it back to the camera. Since the final photo was to show the engine alone against a pure white background, this technique eliminated a lot of difficult blocking out on the negative of background behind the detailed parts of the valve gear, etc.

Jardine was an experimenter, and when the new Kodachrome color slide film was released he, of course, tried it. Thus we have the two beautiful photos shown here, taken by Don with his personal camera, at the time of the 4436's portrait session.

An excellent article on Don and his techniques and accomplishments appears in the February 1977 issue of *Trains* Magazine. Don wasn't the only member of the Jardine family to achieve fame. Younger son Alan became a member of the Beach Boys singing group.

*After Lima's photographer Don Jardine made the black and white 7 x 17 and 8 x 10 size negatives of GS-4 4436 for the company, he did a little photography for himself. In 1941, Kodachrome was still a new phenomenon, having only been introduced a couple of years earlier. Don tried it out on the freshly built Daylight with spectacular results. (Don Jardine photo)*

*The bright colors of brand new Daylight number 4436 contrast with the dull factory colors of its birthplace, Lima Locomotive Works. Don Jardine photographed the streamliner's face on 35mm Kodachrome film, which was very small compared to the large sheet film black and white negatives he made for his employer. (Don Jardine photo)*

*Brand spanking new GS-2 number 4415 has just arrived at East St. Louis from Lima on January 3, 1937. The sign affixed to the handrail proudly proclaims "Built By Lima Locomotive Works, Inc., Lima, Ohio." Soon the beautiful locomotive will go to Los Angeles to be set up for operation along with its five GS-2 sisters. (Arnold Menke collection)*

*The GS-2 number 4412 has just completed the first test run of the Daylight train on March 1, 1937. Photo taken at Los Angeles. (Leon Callaway collection)*

inauguration of his dream, the southbound Daylight, now numbered 98. In Los Angeles, movie actress Olivia de-Havilland was the honored guest who splashed champagne over #4411's pilot as it began number 99's trip northward. Trains 71 and 72 now became the Coast Passenger, a mail, express, coach, and lunch car heavyweight.

Popularity of the new streamlined Daylight trains was almost instantaneous. Ridership increased markedly, proving the validity of McDonald's

It hailed the $136,000 4-8-4s as "being particularly designed to attain greater speeds than any previous passenger engine used by Southern Pacific."

In early 1937 the six GS-2s arrived in Los Angeles from Lima and were given break-in runs and tests on conventional trains. The passenger car trainsets arrived in California a little later. Together with the new locomotives they went on a whirlwind tour of 12 cities for public display.

## Launching the Daylights

On March 21, 1937, the new streamlined Daylights were christened in a ceremony that was broadcast on NBC radio. President McDonald was on hand in San Francisco to see the

*The 4411 is having its first southbound run with the Daylight in this action photo taken by Gerald M. Best in early 1937. (Kenneth G. Johnsen collection)*

---

GS-3 4416 speeds the heavyweight Coast Passenger train north of Burbank Junction on November 10, 1937. (Gerald M. Best photo)

Heading for Los Angeles, the Morning Daylight storms out of San Francisco in 1937. (Southern Pacific Company)

theories. As more equipment became available, additional service was offered. On March 30, 1940, the Noon Daylight, trains 96 and 97, was added. Numbers 98 and 99 at this time were called the Morning Daylight.

The outbreak of World War II brought changes to the passenger service on S.P. In January of 1942 a number of passenger trains were discontinued, including the Noon Daylight, to enable greater capacity for the movement of troops. Numbers 98 and 99 continued to operate, now called

GS-3 4428 begins its journey from Los Angeles to San Francisco with train Number 99, the Coast Daylight. (Southern Pacific Company)

Barely distinguishable under all the flags, bunting, and placards is the number of the locomotive Southern Pacific sent to Los Angeles Union Passenger Terminal's grand opening: 4426.

The opening of Los Angeles Union Passenger Terminal in 1939 was celebrated with a "Romance of the Rails" spectacle. Santa Fe sent a 2-10-4, Union Pacific sent a 4-6-6-4 Challenger, and Southern Pacific sent one of their new Daylights, bedecked from stem to stern in a sea of flags. (Richard Lohse collection)

This Southern Pacific ad proudly announces the new Daylight train and all its amenities. (Richard Lohse collection)

The Daylight was less than a year old when this ad came out touting the popularity of the streamlined train. (Richard Lohse collection)

GS-4 4442 powers the Noon Daylight in Simi Valley at Hassan in November 1947. (Jack Woods photo from the collection of Tom Gildersleeve)

The 4456 bursts out of the Lower Chatsworth Tunnel in 1946. (Fred Ragsdale photo from the collection of Guy Denechaud)

the Coast Daylight. The Coast Passenger, numbers 71 and 72, became night trains.

After war's end, the railroad in April of 1946 restored the Noon Daylight (96 and 97), renamed 98 and 99 the Morning Daylight, and restored 71 and 72 to daytime service. Sufficient numbers of streamlined GS locomotives were now on hand to handle the traffic. The Coast Daylight and the Coast Passenger's schedules coincided at Santa Barbara and frequently two gleaming streamlined GS engines would park side by side there as the former passed the latter.

By 1949 the passenger situation was changing due to competition from automobiles and airlines. In October of that year the Noon Daylight was discontinued for the final time. Its equipment was transferred to the night coach train, the Starlight. It wasn't long

Continued on page 27

The new and the old: 4-8-4 and 4-8-2 meet in Santa Barbara on the Coast Daylight and the Coast Passenger, respectively. (Robert B. McNeel photo)

Night stop at Santa Barbara. The 4433 has an interesting paint scheme for a GS-4. It still has its skirts, but it is apparently all black like the Warbaby paint scheme, yet it has the newer (after 1946) lettering on the tender. (Robert B. McNeel photo)

One of the original Daylight locomotives of 1937, GS-2 number 4412, is in charge of train number 72, the Coast Passenger, at Somis, California, in the late 1940s. Ralph Lettelier took the photo. (Alan Miller collection)

The meet between the Coast Daylight and the Coast Passenger at Santa Barbara sometimes produced stunning images such as this one of the 4441 and 4448 side by side. (Robert B. McNeel photo)

A couple of early colorized postcards promoting the Noon Daylight and the Coast Daylight. The upper view is an obvious reversal of the original photograph; note which side of the smokebox door has the hinges. (Kenneth G. Johnsen collection)

Future famous GS-4 4449 storms out of San Francisco with the Morning Daylight on March 16, 1952. (Wilbur Whittaker photo)

Southbound (eastbound by S.P. parlance) Coast Daylight, train Number 98, photographed by Ralph Lettelier in the late 1940s at Moorpark. (Alan Miller collection)

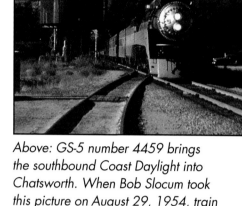

Above: GS-5 number 4459 brings the southbound Coast Daylight into Chatsworth. When Bob Slocum took this picture on August 29, 1954, train Number 98 was just a few months away from dieselization. (Bob Slocum photo)

Left: The 4451 has number 76, the Lark Pullman train at Glendale in the early 1950s. (Bill Olson photo)

The Noon Daylight leaves Los Angeles Union Passenger Terminal behind GS-4 number 4442 in January of 1940. (Jack Woods photo from the collection of Tom Gildersleeve)

*Future celebrity 4449 backs down to Los Angeles Union Passenger Terminal to get the Sunset Limited in a beautiful photo by Jack Woods in January of 1948. At one time or another Daylight locomotives could be seen on nearly every name train and division on the Southern Pacific. (Jack Woods photo from the collection of Tom Gildersleeve)*

*In the halcyon days of steam, the shops and roundhouses of the S.P. were fascinating places for fathers and sons to visit. No one chased you out; no one cared if you took pictures. And a friendly hostler might even give you a short cab ride. This photo of the roundhouse in Los Angeles, taken by Jack Woods in April of 1949, is so evocative of the visits made to the same spot by my dad and myself many moons ago. (Tom Gildersleeve collection)*

before the Starlight itself was cancelled and the long downward spiral toward Amtrak began.

Southern Pacific passenger service grew in the San Joaquin Valley of California, as did its Coast Line counterparts. In 1927 the railroad had launched the San Joaquin Flyer with heavyweight equipment. When, in 1941, new equipment purchases for the streamlined Coast Daylight freed up some of its first-generation streamlined equipment, the time was ripe to upgrade the San Joaquin to Daylight status.

GS 4-8-4s were more than enough power for trains Number 51 and 52, the newly streamlined San Joaquin Daylight, so 4-6-2 Pacific type locomotives were used at first. Three of

The 4457, still in Daylight dress, heads the southbound mail train Number 72 at San Luis Obispo on July 4, 1954. (Bob Slocum photo)

To dress up the new San Joaquin Daylight with something resembling streamlined equipment, Southern Pacific's Los Angeles shops dolled up three booster-equipped P-10 Pacifics, numbers 2484, 2485, and 2486 and assigned them to the train. Skirting and skyline casings, as well as the niftiest paint scheme ever to grace a Vanderbilt tender, gave the San Joaquins a racy look. Photo was taken on July 4, 1941, the first day of operation of the new train. (Wilbur Whittaker photo)

The 4452 rolls along with the mail train Number 90 near Santa Susana on October 3, 1955. (John Hungerford photo from the collection of Tom Moungovan)

them were given streamlined side skirting and skyline casings, and painted in the red, orange, and black paint scheme of the Daylights. Service began on July 4, 1941.

Postwar increases in traffic, as well as displaced equipment from Coast Line upgrades, allowed expansion of the San Joaquin Daylights and eventually resulted in the need for bigger steam power in the form of MT 4-8-2 types and GS 4-8-4 types. For a while, Alco PAs were used on the San Joaquin Daylight before relinquishing it back to the GS Daylight steam engines, making 51 and 52 the last long-haul steam powered passenger trains on the Southern Pacific.

The Northbound Coaster makes its stop at Glendale in the mid-1940s. (Ralph Lettelier photo from the collection of Alan Miller)

Early color photo of one of the San Joaquin Daylight Pacifics. (Steve Peery collection)

The northbound San Joaquin Daylight has a 4-8-2 helper in Soledad Canyon in the mid-1940s. (Ralph Lettelier photo from the collection of Alan Miller)

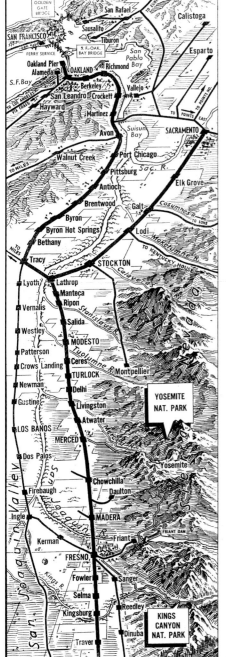

In the charge of a GS-6, the northbound San Joaquin Daylight, train Number 51, winds through the hills near Russ in 1948. (Ralph Lettelier photo from the collection of Alan Miller)

This map of the San Joaquin Valley Route from Los Angeles to Oakland, along with descriptions of towns along the way, was given to passengers on the San Joaquin Daylight (and its short Sacramento Daylight connecting train) in a brochure called "Your Daylight Trip." (Kenneth G. Johnsen collection)

AC-10 cab forward 4217, representing Southern Pacific's other most famous type of steam locomotive, waits in the hole for the San Joaquin Daylight to pass. The 4464 has Number 51 in tow at Palmdale in this 1948 photo by Stanley Snook. (Jim Harrison collection)

## The Daylights' Extended Family

Although the streamlined Daylight locomotives were Pacific Lines engines, their fame and striking good looks did not go unnoticed on Southern Pacific's Texas subsidiary, Texas & New Orleans. In July of 1937 the T&NO leased three Pacific Lines 4-6-2 Pacific types and took them into their Houston shops for a radical makeover.

The streamlined engines that emerged and went into service in September of that year looked for all the world like the Daylights' little sisters. A cone-shaped nose on the smokebox front, streamlined pilot and shroud, side skirting, and full skyline casing replicated the Daylight look for Texans. Not called Daylights, the streamliners were Numbers 13 and 25, the Sunbeam and Hustler, which held down a fast schedule between Dallas and Houston.

Daylight copycat T&NO Sunbeam was a Pacific Lines 4-6-2 in Daylight dress. The Sunbeam is leaving Houston in 1953. (Joe R. Thompson)

The Daylight locomotives had a couple other distant relatives, which should be mentioned here. During World War II the government controlled the construction and allocation of locomotives to fit the needs

Competition from Burlington's Sam Houston Zephyr induced Southern Pacific subsidiary T&NO to obtain three P-6 4-6-2 Pacifics (numbers 2455, 2456, and 2457) and dress them up like Daylights in the Houston shops. The treatment was more complete than S.P. had done with the San Joaquins. A streamlined pilot and shroud and Boxpok drivers were among the improvements made. They became engine numbers 650, 651, and 652 in Texas. (Harold K. Vollrath collection)

of the war effort. When Southern Pacific placed the order with Lima Locomotive Works for the GS-6 Class, the War Production Board allocated some of the series to the Western Pacific. Those engines are covered in Chapter 3. But at this same time, the Central of Georgia needed some heavy power, and so a sort of knockoff of the GS-6 was designed for them by Lima. It bore no streamlining at all and did not have a booster engine, but otherwise was basically the same steam locomotive.

Southern Pacific was known for its famous cab forward 4-8-8-2 articulated locomotives. A slightly lesser known, yet equally impressive articulated class, the 2-8-8-4 AC-9, was built by Lima in late 1939. These 12 Yellowstone types were built as coal burners for use in the Southwest. Later in their lives they operated in Nevada and Northern California and were converted to oil burners. What distinguishes them is the streamlining that Lima applied in the form of a full skyline casing and the same streamlined pilots as used on the Daylights. Numbered in the

The look is one of brute strength, yet there are refinements visible that were possessed by no other articulated locomotives on the rails. S.P.'s AC-9 Class 2-8-8-4 locomotives sported full skyline casings and streamlined pilots that were identical to those of the Daylights. Originally coal burners, they were converted to burn oil in later years. Photo shows a railfan excursion on the Modoc Line in 1954. (Jim Harrison collection)

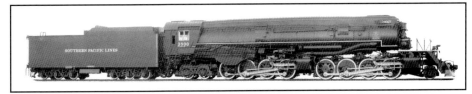

Builder photo of S.P. AC-9 2-8-8-4 semi-streamlined articulated locomotive number 3800. Lima built 12 of the enclosed-cab brutes for the Southern Pacific during the same time it built the Daylights. (Allen County Historical Society collection)

3800s, the AC-9s were the railroad's—and the country's—only streamlined articulated locomotives. If the T&NO Sunbeams were the Daylights' little sisters, the Yellowstones were certainly their big brothers.

Those who were lucky enough to live during the roughly 20-year reign of the GS Daylight locomotives surely have an indelible memory of these great machines. For a person who was not yet born by the time the Daylights ended their service, it can sometimes be difficult to distinguish one model from another. Hence a primer—or Daylight Spotter's Guide—is presented here:

Viewed from the front, the number and arrangement of headlights is the easiest spotting feature. The GS-2s, GS-3s, and GS-6s had a single headlight mounted in the center of the smokebox door. The GS-2s and GS-3s had an open-backed cab, with the ladder mounted on the tender. The

GS-6s had an enclosed, all-weather cab with the ladder mounted on the engine. The GS-2s and GS-3s came from the builder with their train number indicator boards mounted on the skyline casing beside the smokestack. The GS-6s were built with the indicator boards located midway back along the skyline casing for easier readability. Later, the GS-2s and GS-3s had their boards moved back also.

The classic GS-2 features single headlight, smaller drivers, and open cab with steps on tender. Number 4410 is pictured on its break-in run at Los Angeles on January 15, 1937. The engine is so new that many of its tires still carry the white paint applied by the builder. This would soon go away. (Gerald M. Best photo)

GS-3 locomotive in a pleasing portrait taken by a company photographer when the engine was still in its prime. The only noticeable difference from a GS-2 is in the larger size of the drivers. (Southern Pacific Company)

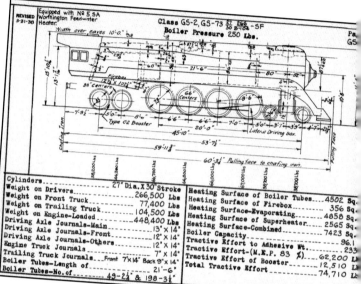

Southern Pacific Company official diagram for the Class GS-2. (Richard Lohse collection)

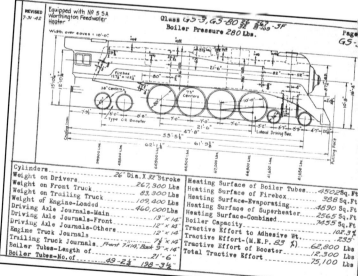

Southern Pacific Company official diagram for the Class GS-3. (Richard Lohse collection)

The platform above the pilot on a GS-6 was the same rounded type as on the GS-4 and GS-5. Pilot platforms on the GS-2s and GS-3s were squared off. The GS-6s came from the builder black and without skirts. The GS-2s and GS-3s had skirting and red and orange paint when new. In later years they were painted black and lost their side skirting. The skirting was cut off, leaving enough material to support the pilot steps. The cut side of the steps left a roundish shape near the top, which differs from the straight-line sides of the GS-6 steps.

The GS-2s and GS-6s had 73-inch drivers. The GS-3s, GS-4s, and GS-5s had 80-inch drivers. Thus the quickest and primary spotting difference between a GS-2 and a GS-3 is the size of the drivers. The smaller drivers, single headlight, and lack of side skirting differentiate the GS-6s from the GS-4s and GS-5s.

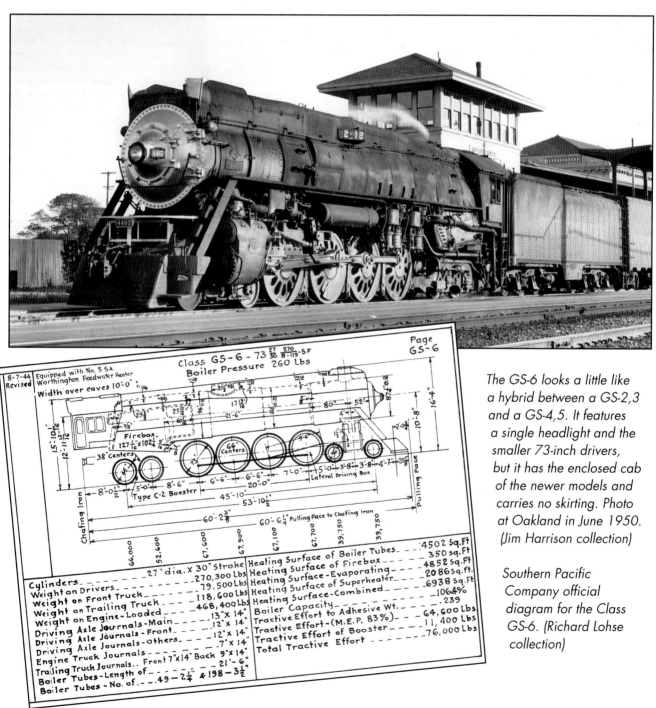

*The GS-6 looks a little like a hybrid between a GS-2,3 and a GS-4,5. It features a single headlight and the smaller 73-inch drivers, but it has the enclosed cab of the newer models and carries no skirting. Photo at Oakland in June 1950. (Jim Harrison collection)*

*Southern Pacific Company official diagram for the Class GS-6. (Richard Lohse collection)*

# Daylight Spotter's Guide cont.

*The classic GS-4, represented by future celebrity 4449, is seen at Glendale on its first Noon Daylight run, July 4, 1941. Quickest spotting feature is the two-headlight smokebox front. The enclosed cab on a red and orange engine also says GS-4 or GS-5. (Gerald M. Best photo)*

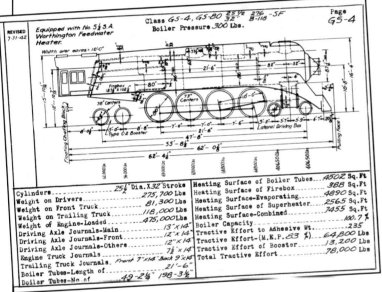

*Southern Pacific Company official diagram for the Class GS-4. (Richard Lohse collection)*

*A Daylight with a black pilot, no skirting, but a red and orange cab will always be a GS-4. Photo at Los Angeles on May 7, 1950. (Al Augenstein photo)*

The GS-4 and GS-5 locomotives have a look all their own and are perhaps the most recognized of the Daylights because of the popularity of their sole surviving example, the 4449. GS-4s and GS-5s have both a headlight and a Mars light mounted one above the other on the smokebox door, which is their easiest distinguishing feature. They have all-weather cabs and were built new with skirting on the sides. The GS-4s were built in two groups, the first consisting of engine numbers 4430 through 4449, and the second order consisting of engine numbers 4450 through 4457. Members of the first group look just like members of the second group. The two GS-5s were built in the same order as the second group.

The easiest way to distinguish a GS-5 from a GS-4 is to look at the journals on the trailer truck. The two GS-5s were fully roller bearing-equipped and have the round bolted-on cover characteristic of roller bearing journals. The GS-4s have lids on the journals that can be flipped open in the manner of old friction-bearing journals. (An exception to this is today's 4449, which has been retrofitted with roller bearings in its trailer truck. The original friction bearing lids were left in place to keep its appearance consistent with the GS-4 Class.) Also, Southern Pacific painted little stars on the driver axles of friction bearing locomotives and a round roller bearing symbol on the driver axles of roller bearing locomotives.

*The classic GS-5 is almost indistinguishable from the GS-4 except for one small detail: the journal covers on its trailer truck are the round lids of roller bearing journals. Both GS-5s were all roller bearing engines. Photo date: March 31, 1947. (Bill Bassler photo)*

Viewed from behind, the tender and cab are the primary spotting features. The GS-2s and GS-3s had tenders whose water compartments were squared off at the top. The ladders for climbing into the open cabs were mounted on the front of these tenders. The GS-4s, GS-5s, and GS-6s

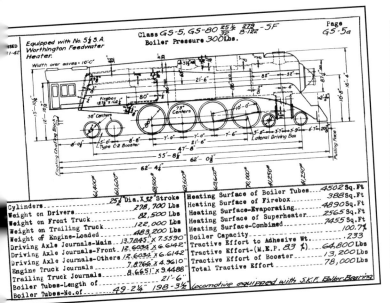

*Southern Pacific Company official diagram for the Class GS-5 (S.K.F.). (Richard Lohse collection)*

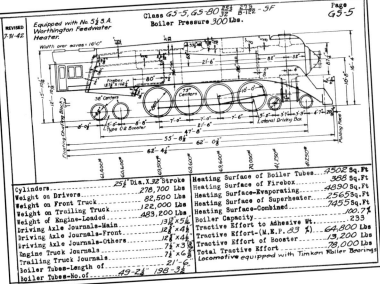

*Southern Pacific Company official diagram for the Class GS-5 (Timken). (Richard Lohse collection)*

*Detail view of the open cab and tender of a GS-3. (Southern Pacific Company)*

*Classic servicing shot at Bakersfield in 1955 compares the two types of Daylight tenders.*
*The one on the left has a more rounded top that blends with the contours of the Daylight's passenger cars. This type was used on the Classes GS-4, GS-5, and GS-6. The one on the right is more squared off on top and is representative of the type used on the first two classes of GS engine. (Tom King photo)*

had tenders, which were more rounded at the top, to blend in with the shape of the passenger cars they pulled. Open cab backs characterized the GS-2s and GS-3s; enclosed cabs were featured on the GS-4s, GS-5s, and GS-6s.

At one time or another all Daylight engines were black. But if they were red and orange, they had to be a GS-2 through GS-5. If they were red and orange on the tender and cab only, they were a GS-4 in the early 1950s. If they were red, white, and blue, they were a specific GS-4—the 4449!

When new, Western Pacific's Daylights closely resembled an S.P. GS-6 except for the feather on the tender. Soon after Western Pacific placed these engines into service, they decided to add elephant-ear-type smoke deflectors. This is the primary spotting feature of a Western Pacific Daylight locomotive and is immediately recognizable. W.P. Number

# Daylight Spotter's Guide cont.

*Rear view of the 4430 at Bakersfield in 1955. The boxy enclosed cab and large drivers identify this engine to be a GS-4 (or 5). Close inspection of the tender reveals the stripes under the black paint that used to be red and orange. (Tom King photo)*

*Rear view of the 4411 shows the GS-2 tender and open cab. These plus the skirting on the side lets us know it is not a GS-6. Photo by Jack Woods at Los Angeles in April of 1949. (Tom Gildersleeve collection)*

482 has an additional spotting feature: a hybrid smokebox front. The center door is a Lima streamlined Daylight type with the headlight built in. But the large front lid is clearly off of some other locomotive because it is much flatter. This resulted from a wreck in Nevada.

So now a quiz to see if you've been paying attention: You see a photo of a black, skirtless, single headlight S.P. Daylight on a freight taken in 1956. Quick, is it a GS-2, a GS-3, or a GS-6? Answer: If it has an enclosed cab, it's a GS-6. If it has large 80-inch drivers, it's a GS-3. If it has neither, it's a GS-2. Congratulations, you passed!

*Except for the feather on the tender and the white stripe on the running board, early Western Pacific GS engines looked very much like their Southern Pacific counterparts. Engine number 483 is seen at Oroville, California, on August 2, 1947. (Jim Boynton photo)*

*An almost classic look of a Western Pacific Daylight engine. The one thing that sets 482 apart from its brethren is the non-Lima smokebox front. It acquired the unusual face as a result of a bad accident it was involved in at Pilot, Nevada. The elephant-ear smoke lifters were a Western Pacific addition to all six of its GS engines. Photo was taken at Stockton on June 23, 1950. (Jim Boynton photo)*

# Daylight Locomotive Specifications

| Railroad Numbers | S.P. 4410-4415 | S.P. 4416-4429 | S.P. 4430-4457 | S.P. 4458-4459 | S.P. 4460-4469 | W.P. 481-486 |
|---|---|---|---|---|---|---|
| Railroad Class | GS-2 | GS-3 | GS-4 | GS-5 | GS-6 | 481 |
| Cylinders, Bore & Stroke | 27″ x 30″ | 26″ x 32″ | 25½″ x 32″ | 25½″ x 32″ | 27″ x 30″ | 27″ x 30″ |
| Drivers, Diameter | 73″ | 80″ | 80″ | 80″ | 73″ | 73″ |
| Boiler Pressure | 250 lbs. | 280 lbs. | 300 lbs. | 300 lbs. | 260 lbs. | 260 lbs. |
| Tractive Effort, Cylinders | 62,200 lbs. | 62,800 lbs. | 64,800 lbs. | 64,800 lbs. | 64,600 lbs. | 64,200 lbs. |
| Tractive Effort, Booster | 12,500 lbs. | 12,300 lbs. | 13,200 lbs. | 13,200 lbs. | 11,450 lbs. | 11,300 lbs. |
| Tractive Effort, Total | 74,700 lbs. | 75,100 lbs. | 78,000 lbs. | 78,000 lbs. | 76,050 lbs. | 75,500 lbs. |
| Boiler Diameter, Front | 86″ | 86″ | 86″ | 86″ | 86″ | 86″ |
| Boiler Diameter, Rear | 96″ | 96″ | 96″ | 96″ | 96″ | 96″ |
| Firebox Size | 127″ x 102¼″ | 127″ x 102¼″ | 127″ x 102¼″ | 127″ x 102¼″ | 127 1/16″ x 102¼″ | 127 1/16″ x 102¼ |
| Wheelbase, Drivers | 20′ 0″ | 21′ 6″ | 21′ 6″ | 21′ 6″ | 20′ 0″ | 20′ 0″ |
| Wheelbase, Engine | 45′ 10″ | 47′ 8″ | 47′ 8″ | 47′ 8″ | 45′ 10″ | 45′ 10″ |
| Wheelbase, Engine & Tender | 94′ ½″ | 95′ 10½″ | 96′ 3″ | 96′ 3″ | 94′ 5″ | 94′ 5″ |
| Overall Length, Engine & Tender | 107′ 11¾″ | 109′ 9¾″ | 110′ 2¼″ | 110′ 2¼″ | 109′ 0″ | 109′ 0″ |
| Weight on Drivers | 266,500 lbs. | 267,300 lbs. | 275,700 lbs. | 275,700 lbs. | 270,300 lbs. | 280,950 lbs. |
| Weight, Engine Loaded | 448,400 lbs. | 460,000 lbs. | 475,000 lbs. | 475,000 lbs. | 468,400 lbs. | 466,100 lbs. |
| Tender Capacity, Water | 22,000 gals. | 22,000 gals. | 23,300 gals. | 23,300 gals. | 23,300 gals. | 23,300 gals. |
| Tender Capacity, Oil | 6,010 gals. | 6,010 gals. | 5,880 gals. | 5,880 gals. | 5,880 gals. | 6,000 gals. |

CHAPTER TWO

# DAYLIGHT MECHANICAL DETAILS AND OPERATION

Doyle McCormack on April 25, 1981, ready to head to Sacramento's Railfair '81. If credit can go to any one man above all the others for bringing the 4449 back to life and for keeping it in excellent condition, it must go to this knowledgeable man.

*To a kid at trackside, the man at the controls in the cab of a Daylight had the status of some sort of god. He who could tame this seemingly living beast must have extraordinary powers. He was also darned lucky too!*

*Most of the S.P. hoggers who ran the Daylights, over 50 years ago, have gone on to their reward. And the Daylights they operated lasted only 15 to 20 years in service on Southern Pacific before they too met their fate. But one man and one engine have been together over 30 years and it is safe to say they know each other intimately. Doyle McCormack headed the team that rebuilt S.P. 4449 for the American Freedom Train in 1975 and he has been its engineer ever since.*

*To be able to run the engine, one must understand its parts and what they do. In this chapter, Doyle, the undisputed authority on Daylights, explains the components of GS-4 #4449 that bring it to life:*

## "Ask the Man Who Owns One"

Let's start with the main engine. It is a one-piece steel frame from front to back. The cylinders are cast with the frame. The bottom chamber is the main piston and the top chamber is the valve assembly. The piston rod connects to the crosshead, which moves in the crosshead guide.

The levers, or Walschaerts valve gear linkage, consist of the eccentric crank which is offset 90 degrees from the axis and gives you the position you need to work the valves. It's like a camshaft in your car. When the engine is parked with the rods down, the crank is at a 45-degree angle. That gives you the lead you need to make the whole thing function.

The link and link block is used by the engineer to set the engine in

Eccentric crank on 4449.

*Ad for Alco power reverse. Items such as these were vendor items that could be found on a variety of steam engines. (Fred Spurrell collection)*

forward or reverse. He sets it by means of an air-assisted power reverse lever in the cab. Linkage in the lower portion of the link block is forward and in the upper half is reverse.

For forward motion, the engineer pushes the lever forward and this pushes the link down in the link block, which gives the valve the travel it needs. The further toward the outer limits of the block you go, the further the travel of the valve. The shorter the stroke of the valve, the less time the valve is open.

When the engine is starting out, the valve lets steam in front of the piston and pushes it back. Then the valve shifts, puts steam in the back, and exhausts steam out the front. As you get going faster and faster, you don't leave the valve open for the full stroke. During the part of the stroke where the valve closes, the steam expands and does its work. Then when the valve shifts, the pressure on the back side of the piston is minimal. If you left it at full stroke, when the valve shifted you'd have full boiler pressure on one side and full boiler pressure on the other side and hence no power. You get power when you have a differential in pressure.

So as you're going down the railroad, you move it one notch at a time, up and up and up. (The engineer can hear it in the stack.) When you're going 80 miles an hour, you're getting very little travel in the valve. The smaller vertical valve lever gives you what is called the lap and lead and keeps it all synchronized correctly.

There are two lubricators located above the valve gear on the locomotive's right side. The valve oil lubricator provides lubrication to the cylinders and the valves. It uses steam oil, which has a very high flash point and is pretty stiff oil. The car oil lubricator supplies oil to a lot of the running gear like the shoes and wedges, the driving boxes, and all the wear surfaces on the running gear itself. It takes the place of the engineer going around the engine with his long

spout oiler. Each line goes to a splitter, which divides it four ways. So every line feeds four points of lubrication.

## Making Steam

Back from the drivers is the blowdown muffler. As you evaporate water out of a boiler making steam, it only evaporates the pure water. Everything else that's in the water stays behind and collects in the boiler. This engine will go through 20,000 gallons of water pretty quickly. When we make a 300-mile trip, we figure we're going to use 30 to 35 thousand gallons of water or more. When you evaporate 30,000 gallons of water it leaves a lot of crud behind and it all collects in the lower end of the firebox called the mud ring.

In the cab is a lever that operates the blowdown valve. It lets the collected crud out of the boiler. But you don't want to shoot it out at some poor soul standing by the track, so it goes through a pipe and is dispersed at trackside through the blowdown mufflers.

The firebox has two walls, inner and outer, with water between them. The mud ring is the ring around the very bottom part of the firebox where everything eventually settles. There are

*Blowdown muffler on 4449.*

washout plug at mud ring

*Washout plug at mud ring on 4449.*

34 washout plugs on the engine, which you remove when you wash out the boiler. All the crud comes out through them. We do this every 31 days.

The trailer truck has the booster engine. It surrounds the rear axle. A two-cylinder steam engine lies on its side in the trailer truck. It is a fixed cutoff engine. It doesn't have a reverse gear—it only works in forward motion. It is connected to a crankshaft, which has a gear that gets engaged to the bull gear on the rear axle of the trailer truck by means of an air-actuated idler gear. You get 13,000 pounds of added tractive effort.

There is no clutch; it just slams in, so usually you kick in the booster while you're standing still. It helps only up to 21 miles per hour. The booster goes at a higher RPM than the main engine. So when you have the booster kicked in, it likes a lot of steam and water! Exhaust from the booster engine goes down a pipe from the engineer's side. The supply is on the fireman's side.

The frame sits on a heart rocker, which allows the trailer truck to move under the back of the engine when you're going around a curve. All of the spring rigging on the trailer truck is interlaced with the rigging on the rest of the engine and distributes the load evenly.

Taking in slack going around curves is somewhat difficult for the drivers, which have no blind wheels. There's a certain amount of lateral movement in the wheels themselves that allow the

# Sidelined by a Soft Plug

Southern Pacific developed and manufactured its own fusible plugs for the locomotives' crown sheets. If the water got to within six inches above the crown sheet, the rising temperature would melt the center of the plug, allowing steam to blow through the firebox. This was a very serious matter and resulted in immediate suspension for the person responsible. Fireman Bob McNeel relates one such incident:

The 4448 was on #25 on the night of October 16, 1942, with Ray Bates as engineer. He was an elderly gentleman with many years of engine service. He had never had an accident or a reprimand. He was one of the old school of loyal railroaders.

This trip the 4448 dropped a soft plug between Palmdale and Lancaster. I was sent deadheading on #55 the evening of the 17th to messenger the engine back in to Taylor Shops. As I carried my old pocket Kodak with me everywhere in those days, I took this picture of the 4448 on the siding at Palmdale early on the morning of the 18th. She was placed in the train of the eastbound Mojave-L.A. local, and

*S.P. 4448 dropped a soft plug and was sidelined at Palmdale for a ride back to the shops in the middle of a freight train. (Robert B. McNeel photo)*

at stops I was to lubricate her and ride her to see that no bearings got hot.

Ray Bates was pulled out of service and he became very depressed. Later on he was exonerated of any fault as they discovered through tests that the soft plugs were faulty and the cause of the failure was <u>not</u> low water. Ray died shortly after this incident. He felt the company had treated him unfairly.

*Southern Pacific manufactured its own soft plugs because they were an S.P. invention. Racks of soft plugs are seen here ready for installation in S.P. steam locomotives. (Richard Lohse collection)*

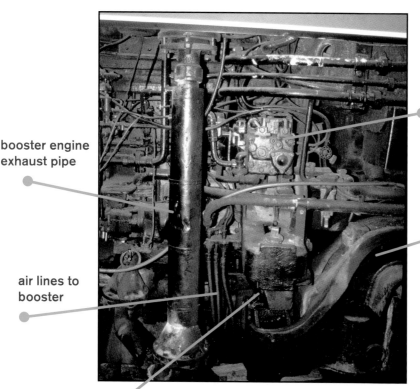

booster engine exhaust pipe

air control valve

air lines to booster

trailer truck

heart rocker

*View under engineer's side of the cab.*

injecto

*Nathan injector on 4449.*

*Ad for the Westinghouse HSC electro-pneumatic brake system on the Daylights. This system allowed very smooth and accurate stops. (Richard Lohse collection)*

axles to move in the frame. The wheelbase is 21 feet. The lead axle has a lateral motion device on it, which allows it to move an inch and a half when it comes into a curve. There are two big springs in it that allow the journal boxes to move from side to side 1-1/2 inches. The 4449 doesn't like it but it will do it. That's when we hear the groans and squeaks.

Also under the cab is a cold water pump, part of the feedwater system. It's a centrifugal pump that takes the water from the tender and pumps it up through the pipe to a heater in the very front of the smokebox. There it combines with the exhaust steam and warms the water. By gravity it goes down to the hot water pump (which is mounted under the skirting above the crosshead guide on the fireman's side up near the front) and it pumps it into the boiler. It is a large reciprocating pump.

There are two systems to feed water into the boiler: the feedwater pump and the injector on the other side. The feedwater pump preheats the water using exhaust steam, so you're capturing some of the energy that

normally would go up the stack as exhaust and imparting that energy to the water as heat and putting it back into the boiler. It gives you 5 to 10 percent energy conservation. The injector just shoots cold water in; the feedwater system can be used to regulate the amount of heat and consequently is easier on the boiler than the injector.

There are two hose connections on the pilot. One is the air brake and one is the signal line. In the days before radios they had an air communication system on passenger trains. There was a whistle in the cab and the conductor could pull a valve in any one of the cars to signal the engineer.

The steam heat connection is only on the back via the tender. Passenger engines were designed to go forward! Some switch engines had steam heat connections on both front and back.

The Westinghouse air pumps on the fireman's side are double-acting cross compound pumps that compress air for the air brake system and the other systems on the engine that require air pressure. They are 150-cfm pumps.

The injector is the other feedwater device that injects water into the boiler. It has no moving parts. It is a series of nozzles that uses the energy of steam to impart velocity, not pressure, into the water. The steam is cooled in the cones and imparts its energy into the water as it comes out the bottom. When the high-speed water hits the check valve, it pushes it open and disperses into the boiler. Boiler pressure pushes the check valve back shut. The check valves are located at the front of the engine because you want to put the colder water at the front of the boiler.

The firing valve controls how much oil is fed into the firebox from the tender. It is all gravity-fed. It goes from the valve through a pipe to the center of the front of the firebox where it enters the burner.

The steam heat line goes first to the tank heater in the tender and then back to the rest of the train. The 4449 uses #5 fuel oil. When we fire up the locomotive, if we don't have steam heat available, we can take a 55-gallon drum of diesel fuel, lift it up with a forklift, connect it to a valve on the fuel line, and fire up the engine using the diesel fuel and compressed air.

During fire-up, the boiler grows over an inch. The only place the boiler is rigidly attached to the frame is at the cylinder saddle. When the boiler grows, it comes back and slides in a trough on the trunnion bearing. There are waist sheets along the boiler that are attached by bolts to the frame. They support the boiler but are allowed to flex. The two greatest forces known to mankind are expansion and contraction. You can't defy them; they will crack mountains.

The 4449 and its tender have roller bearings now on all axles except the drivers. It would cost millions to retrofit the drivers. You'd have to have the wheels pressed off the axles, have new axles and bearing boxes made, and then have the frame machined to take the new boxes. It would be a very expensive project!

Front end of 4449's tender showing the radial buffer and hose connections.

The first roller bearings we put on the 4449 were on the lead truck because it takes a lot of abuse up there as it guides the engine down the track. We had rebuilt it in 1984 and within a couple years it wore out again. The second time we rebuilt it, I had new wheels and axles and boxes for roller bearings made for it. Then we did the tender trucks, then the auxiliary tender, and finally the trailer truck. That's as far as we can go.

The drawbars couple the engine to the tender. The radial buffer has a big spring with a series of wedges that keeps tension between the engine and tender in order to keep it from rattling all the time.

## The Cab is the Heart of the Locomotive's Controls

The cab is somewhat like your house: You have a breaker panel; the cab has a row of valves up on top that are the main shutoff valves for all the appliances on the engine. Every one of them has an operating valve somewhere else.

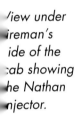

View under fireman's side of the cab showing the Nathan injector.

water valve

injector

steam valve

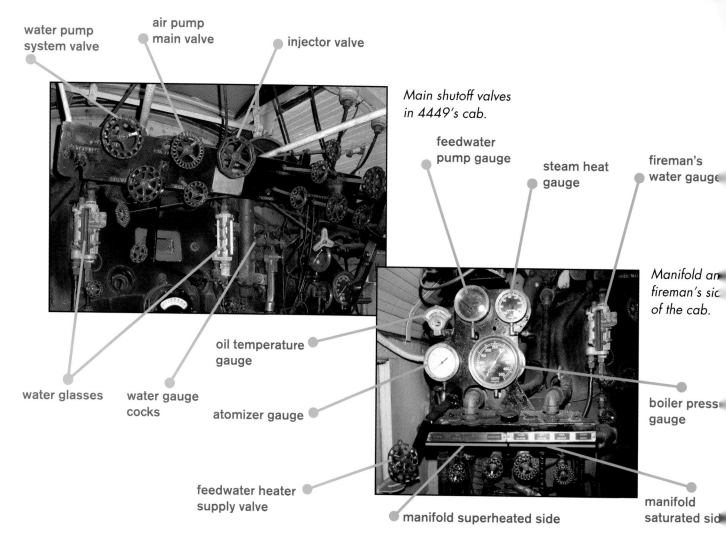

water pump
system valve

air pump
main valve

injector valve

*Main shutoff valves
in 4449's cab.*

feedwater
pump gauge

steam heat
gauge

fireman's
water gauge

*Manifold and
fireman's side
of the cab.*

oil temperature
gauge

water glasses

water gauge
cocks

atomizer gauge

boiler pressure
gauge

feedwater heater
supply valve

manifold superheated side

manifold
saturated side

From left to right is the feedwater pump system valve (the operating valve is located to the left and below it), then the air pump main valve (the operating valves are on each pump), then the injector steam valve (the operating valve is a lever located beside the fireman's seat).

The manifold is located on the fireman's side and is divided. The left half of the manifold is the superheated side and the right half is the saturated side. The shutoff valve for the oil manifold, saturated, is located on the upper right and the one for the oil manifold, superheated, is located on the upper left. Below the manifold are the operating valves for the various things that are run by steam.

From left to right on the manifold are the valves for the blower (in the smokebox), then the heat valve for the line to the feedwater heater so the water doesn't freeze, then the atomizer valve that controls the amount of steam

that goes into the atomizer to blow the oil into the firebox. These, along with the oil valve, are the three main valves that the fireman uses when he's firing the engine.

The three operating valves for the injector are located beside and in front of the fireman's seat box. The valve on the left is the water supply and the one on the right is the overflow.

The wires coming down from above the main shutoff valves come from one of the three turbogenerators to the

gauge lights, the water glass lights, etc. The majority of the electrical system is 32 volt, but the Mars light runs on 12 volts as does the radio and bearing temperature monitoring system. The turbogenerator that was originally used to power the electro-pneumatic brakes is now used for the skirt lights.

The sandbox sits on the floor beneath the fire door into the firebox. When you want to sand the flues (to blow all the soot off the tubes) you flip the little cover open on the fire door,

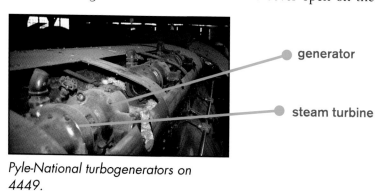

generator

steam turbine

*Pyle-National turbogenerators on
4449.*

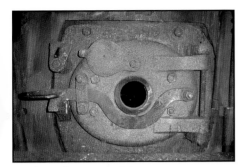

*Firebox door on 4449.*

*Sandbox below firebox door has sand and scoop for "sanding the flues."*

*Water glass on 4449.*

open the sandbox, take a scoop full of sand, and hold it up to the fire door. There is a tremendous amount of suction in there that gathers the sand and blows it through the tubes like a sandblaster. (It also doubles as a kitty litter box if you have to go, but you'd better be on good terms with your fireman!)

There are two water glasses. They are tubular glasses that indicate how much water is in the boiler. Unlike some engines that had a low water alarm, the Daylight doesn't have one. The only alarm you have is when the engine goes BOOM and you don't even have time to bend over and kiss your ass goodbye. It's sort of a short alarm!

The gauge cocks, located beside the water glass, were the original way to test the water level before the invention of the water glass. There are three valves. The engineer would open the bottom one first. If he got water, he knew it was at least that high. Then he would open the next one above and if water came out of it he knew it was at least that high. It was the same for the third valve. It's a foolproof system. If the

water glass should break, what are you going to do? It's another way to monitor the water level in the boiler.

The engineer's side of the cab is the heart of the operation. The reverse gear works the power reverse that positions the valves. It's a servo system. Pushing it forward is for forward movement and pushing it back is for reverse. The pointer is off center when the engine is cold. When you fire the engine up and everything stretches out on the boiler, the pointer is on center in the proper position for operation.

The air brake system is pretty common. You have an engine brake and a train brake. Air brake gauges are located above the handles. The original Daylights had an electro-pneumatic braking system, which electrically controlled the brake valves on each car in

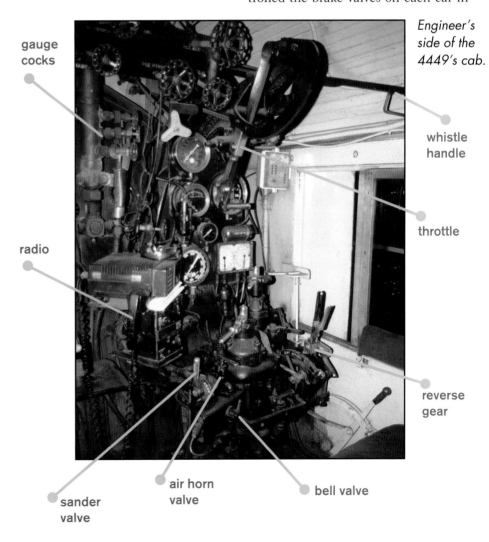

*Engineer's side of the 4449's cab.*

gauge cocks

radio

whistle handle

throttle

reverse gear

sander valve

air horn valve

bell valve

the train, allowing extremely smooth and precise stops. This system is no longer in use.

The big lever above the engineer is the throttle. It opens the throttle valve out on the front of the engine that admits steam into the cylinders. The big gauge above is the steam pressure gauge. It shows your boiler pressure and is marked with a red area at 300 pounds.

Located below and to the left is the backpressure cylinder gauge, which shows how much steam you're admitting into the cylinders from the throttle valve. It's a compound gauge with a little window at the bottom that shows exhaust pressure. If for some reason you can't hear the engine, you can run the engine with that gauge,

but a good engineer doesn't do that—he listens to his engine. There's not supposed to be more than 15 pounds of backpressure.

Beside the steam pressure gauge is the tender water level indicator gauge. And above it is the booster gauge that goes on whenever the booster is engaged.

Hidden down in the corner is the speedometer. The 4449's original speedometer was "liberated" when it was on display in Oaks Park. I brought the current one with me from back east. It's off a Nickel Plate Berkshire. It has a cable that goes down to a drive mechanism that rides on the driver wheel.

The whistle handle is located at the ceiling on the engineer's side. The

air horn, bell, and sander handles are located below and to the left of the brake stands.

The booster valve control works together with the reverse gear. It only works when the gear is in the forward position. A device on the reverse gear is pulled up, causing an air-activated valve to actuate, which engages the gear and opens the booster engine's throttle valve. There is a booster slip control located below the brake stand that can interrupt the supply of air to the throttle valve of the booster without having to shut the main throttle down every time the booster slips.

There is a manual cylinder cock valve in back of the booster valve to let water out of the cylinders.

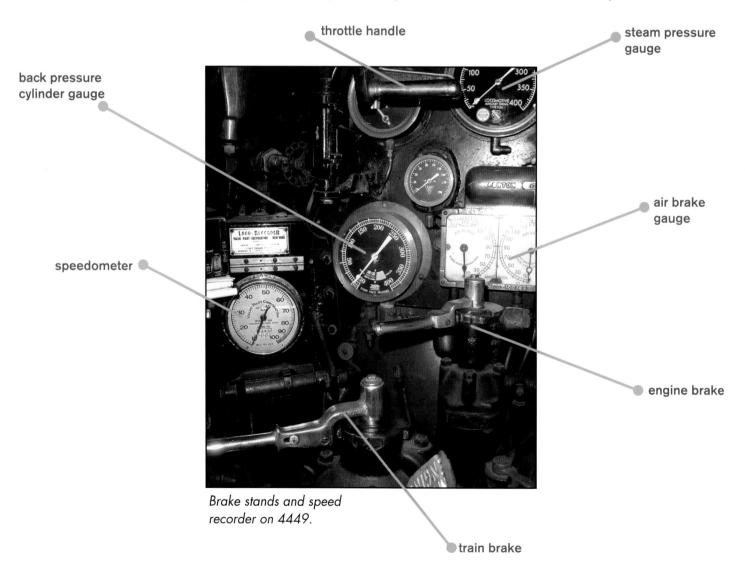

*Brake stands and speed recorder on 4449.*

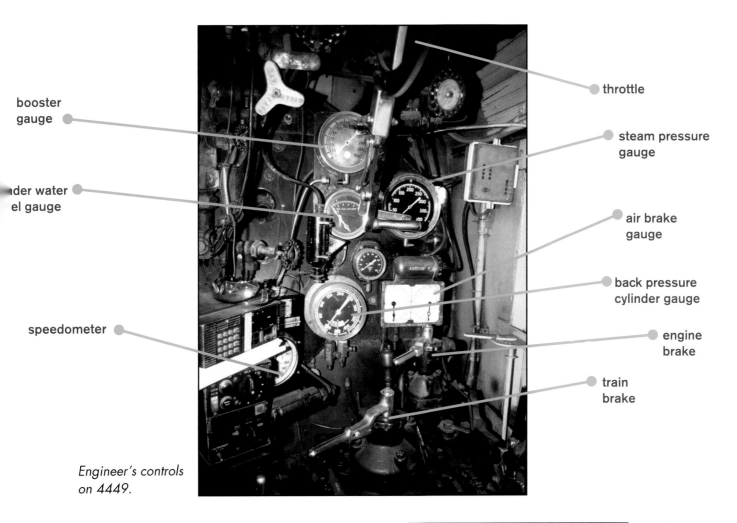

booster gauge

throttle

der water el gauge

steam pressure gauge

air brake gauge

back pressure cylinder gauge

speedometer

engine brake

train brake

*Engineer's controls on 4449.*

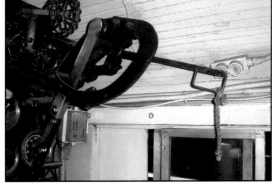

*4449's marine type throttle and whistle lever.*

*Speed recorder and backpressure cylinder gauge on 4449.*

*Boiler pressure gauge on 4449.*

*Water glass and gauge cocks on engineer's side of 4449's cab.*

*Valve Pilot Corporation ad. This device acts as a speedometer and records the engine's speed on a tape. (Richard Lohse collection)*

*The valve pilot has a wheel that contacts the driver wheel's tire and records the revolutions.*

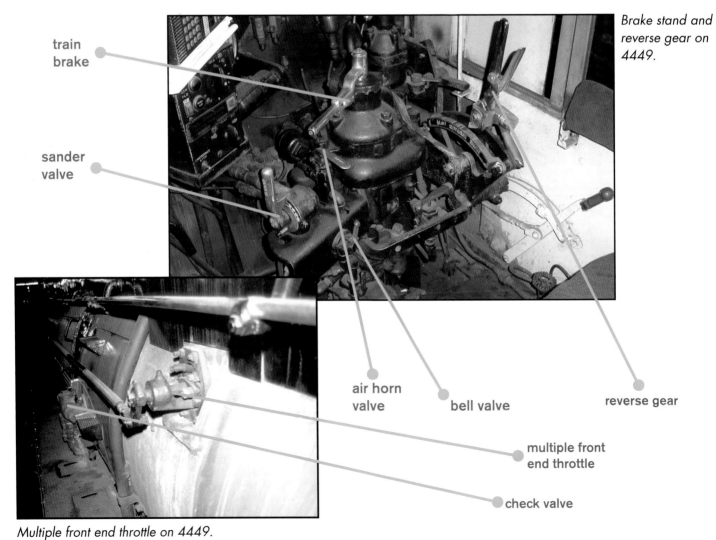

*Brake stand and reverse gear on 4449.*

train brake

sander valve

air horn valve

bell valve

reverse gear

multiple front end throttle

check valve

*Multiple front end throttle on 4449.*

The 4449's original whistle was stolen while the engine sat in Oaks Park, so a replacement from a different GS-4 (on the left) was installed. Another whistle from an S.P.&S. Challenger was donated and mounted on the other side of the stack.

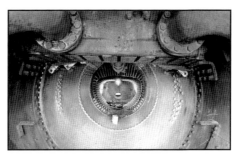

Inside 4449's boiler, looking from the smokebox toward the combustion chamber and firebox.

The lower light on a GS-4 is its headlight; the upper one is its oscillating Mars light.

Smokebox door of 4449 opened to reveal Worthington feedwater heater and associated piping.

The damper valve is connected to a chain by the fireman's feet. It's a hole on the back of the firebox with a door on it. The fireman can pull the chain to let more or less air in for combustion.

The steam heat valve and gauge are located above the manifold on the right side.

The gauge located on the lower left above the manifold is for the atomizer and shows how much steam is being put into the atomizer. Above it in the middle is the feedwater pump gauge, which tells you when the feedwater pump is working. The oil pressure gauge is to the left of the feedwater gauge. And the big gauge located on the lower right above the manifold is the boiler pressure gauge.

The throttle lever goes out to the American Multiple Front End Throttle, which is a series of poppet valves. The throttle lever is connected to a rod that has fingers that open the individual poppet valves to admit more steam in sequence. This setup gives better control and keeps the throttle valve closer to the cylinders so you don't have a steam lag. A bell crank midway takes up the expansion and contraction of the boiler.

The steam dome gives you a high point in the boiler because the steam there is drier and that's what you want. It has a dry pipe that goes through the front tube sheet to the throttle header. It allows you to take the steam out at the highest point in the boiler.

There are three Pyle-National turbogenerators. They are little steam turbines that drive a generator and provide the electricity for the engine. Each one has an operating valve in the cab.

So there you have it. Running the Daylight is not rocket science. It is understanding the machine and how it works.

–Doyle McCormack

## Enginemen Liked the Daylights

The more the engine crews got to know them, the more they understood the "yellow engines." Some said they were as easy to run as a diesel. Firemen said they were as easy to fire as a 4300 Class 4-8-2, long considered to be the best of Southern Pacific's steam engines. The late Robert McNeel had a strong affinity for the Daylights, both as a fireman and as a train photographer:

"I was a fireman on the S.P. in the days of steam from 1935 through 1957 and fired some of the 'yellow bellies.' Most enginemen preferred the GS-3s to any of the other streamliners, I think because they had the 80-inch drivers, but also the open cab. The closed cabs were always too warm most of the year. And photographically, I liked the single headlight of the GS-3s. They just seemed to be a bit more photogenic.

"Of course, most engineers as well as firemen thought the 4300s were the best all around engines the S.P. ever had. We felt the Mountain types would equal the GSs in most areas except at higher speeds. The place where the GS was superior was of course over 75 miles per hour. At those speeds, the Mountains had to be forced a little.

"The GSs were guaranteed originally for 120 miles per hour with a 12-car train, though of course the S.P. never 'officially' allowed more than 79."

## CHAPTER THREE

# WORLD WAR II AND THE DAYLIGHTS

*Warbaby 4449 on turntable at Brooklyn roundhouse in 2000 for S.P.H.&T.S. convention.*

At the dawn of the 1940s, Southern Pacific's Daylight locomotives had already lived up to their design potential and were racking up impressive performance records. They were about to be asked for much, much more.

The most severe test America's railroads have ever faced was during the peak traffic years of World War II. The unprecedented movement of troops, war materials, and machinery strained every U. S. railroad's capacity. Just when it seemed like the limit had been reached, Uncle Sam's war effort demanded even more.

Artwork that appeared in a special issue of the Southern Pacific Bulletin in 1941, devoted entirely to Southern Pacific's role in the country's "gigantic national defense program" following the outbreak of World War II in Europe. (Kenneth G. Johnsen collection)

Southern Pacific Bulletin artwork from a 1941 issue that promoted "how the company's men and women are shouldering their responsibilities" in the defense buildup following the outbreak of war in Europe. (Kenneth G. Johnsen collection)

Locomotives whose service life should have ended by the early 1940s were nursed, cajoled, and otherwise propped up in desperate attempts to wring a few more miles out of them. The nation's railroads had no locomotives to spare, and many an operating department was looking for additional engines to purchase. Shop forces were expanded to minimize the down time of locomotives and other equipment in for repair.

Alco, Baldwin, and Lima, as well as the smaller builders, were stretched to peak production capacity. The government's War Production Board oversaw locomotive production and

developed a plan for allotting locomotives to railroads when and where they were most needed.

As if the strain from domestic production wasn't enough, the builders also had to supply locomotives for export to Europe. Wherever the Allies captured territory, railroading infrastructure had to be rebuilt and locomotives were sorely needed. Factories in war-ravaged Europe were not able to meet demands and thus the American builders were asked to supply motive power.

The East Coast of the United States had not been directly attacked, and although the German war machine was

designing "New York Bombers" there was not an overwhelming sense of fear that the Axis powers would bring the war to our shores. The railroads' war effort consisted of rushing troops and supplies to ports where they would disembark for Europe.

Similarly, Middle America was somewhat insulated from threat of direct attack, and the effort there was one of getting men and materials across the country to ports where they could be shipped out to where they were needed.

But it was a different situation on the West Coast. Not only was there a stronger perceived connection with the air attack on Pearl Harbor in the Hawaiian Islands, but also Japanese submarines had already fired on U. S. territory along the Oregon and California coasts. In addition, Japanese balloon bombs had drifted over the western U. S. and inflicted several casualties. Fears were being justified.

West Coast cities held blackouts and air raid drills, and barrage balloons were hoisted aloft in areas thought to be vulnerable to Japanese air attacks.

Aircraft factories in Southern California and Seattle had huge cloth screens built over them, painted to resemble residential districts from the air. Camouflage became an art during World War II.

## Wartime Strains on the Coast Route

Southern Pacific's Coast Route served more military installations than any other section of railroad in the West. It became a beehive of activity even before the attack on Pearl Harbor as the United States was preparing for the possibility of war. Once the hostilities commenced, the load on the Coast Line intensified. As the focus of the war shifted from Europe to the Pacific, even more pressure was felt on the Coast Line.

S.P. 4449 modeled the "Warbaby" look complete with accurate dispersion shields fabricated by Doyle McCormack. Occasion was the Southern Pacific Historical & Technical Society's convention in Portland, Oregon, in 2000.

Warbaby version of tender exhibited by 4449 in 2000 for the Southern Pacific Historical & Technical Society's meet. Large "Southern Pacific" letters on tender sides did not appear until after World War II in 1946.

Interesting Shell ad with Daylight 4436 on a service station grease rack. Railroads' wartime involvement spawned many interesting ads. (Richard Lohse collection)

Classic Warbaby scheme is modeled by Southern Pacific 4431 at Glendale, California, on November 24, 1943. Dispersion shields have been affixed and all of the red, orange, and silver finery has been painted somber black. (Fred Stindt collection)

In order to free up equipment, as well as track time, the Noon Daylight and the San Francisco to Los Angeles portion of the Sunset Limited were discontinued during the war. Getting enough seats to haul the thousands of troops passing through every week meant pressing every available coach, including commuter coaches, into troop train (Victory Trains, as they were called) service.

At the same time diners and lounge cars were removed from the Coast Line trains and used elsewhere as coach replacements. So acute was the shortage of seat space that Southern Pacific advertisements of the era urged the public <u>not</u> to ride trains unless it was truly necessary.

*Patriotic wartime ad for the Southern Pacific admonishes the reader to buy War Bonds. (Richard Lohse collection)*

*Closeup of 4449's latter day dispersion shield. Note also the bolt pattern on the nose matching the earlier style shield.*

The Coast Line was considered vulnerable to air attack by Japanese planes. Loss or interruption of this vital rail artery to the military could be a crippling blow. Strategists feared a night attack. The headlights of the very trains carrying on the war effort could lead the enemy's bombers to the rail lines.

Thus in early 1942 dispersion shields were applied to locomotive headlights and classification lamps. Instead of the usual half cylindrical shaped visor, dispersion shields were almost conical in shape, with the small end pointed outward. This subdued the view of the headlight from above and limited the amount of light thrown on the tracks ahead of the locomotive. It allowed classification lamps to be viewed from the horizontal, but not from the vertical.

These shields were fabricated at Bayshore Shops and applied to all classes of locomotives, including the Daylights, operating on the West Coast. They became standard on all locos and some signals were even equipped with them.

Interestingly, different types of dispersion shields were experimented

Southern Pacific 4458 with dispersion shields is being set up on the Lidgerwood at Los Angeles to have its tires machined. This mechanism allows the wheels to remain on the locomotive when the tires are reshaped. Wartime miles have added up fast for the nearly new GS-5. (Gerald M. Best photo)

So recently arrived from the builder that its tires are still trimmed in white, 4453 already has the headlight and classification lamp dispersion shields, as well as the iron plate shield welded over the opening in the firebox. Photo at Los Angeles in April of 1942. (Fred Stindt collection)

Still wearing the dispersion shields over its headlight and classification lamps on January 10, 1943, roller bearing-equipped 4459 blasts through Aromas, east of Watsonville Junction with the pride of the Southern Pacific, the westbound (San Francisco bound) Coast Daylight. (Doug Richter collection)

with early on. One type was a much larger hood than the headlight itself. This shield was attached below the Mars light on a GS-4. (The Mars Light was not used during a blackout.) The classification lamps and the lighted number boards on the smokebox front had flat sheet metal awnings mounted over them.

Closeup of an early dispersion shield. The 4449 has a bolt pattern on its nose exactly matching that of this early style shield. Did the 4449 also have a shield at one time? (Fred Stindt collection)

The only photo that has surfaced of this unusual dispersion shield system is of GS-4 4439. However, close inspection of the nose of 4449 reveals a pattern of bolts that exactly matches the early dispersion shield's pattern. Did the 4449 have one of the early shields and then switch to the standard version? 4449 engineer Doyle McCormack thinks so.

Another possibility is that the nose cone from 4439 was swapped with 4449's at some point. It was common practice for parts to be interchanged at shoppings. For example, today's 4449 has the pilot truck from the 4443, the trailer truck from the 4450, and one driver from the 4437, as evidenced by the numbers stamped in each part. However, a close examination of wartime photos of 4449 reveals the characteristic bolt pattern of the early shield on its nose, and so McCormack's hypothesis is probably correct.

Another, less well known, form of camouflaging shield that was applied to the Daylights during wartime was an iron plate welded over the open part of the firebox at the level of the mud ring. This type of plate is still in place on both sides of the 4449. Glow from the firebox was reduced both vertically and horizontally with these shields. Again, the concern was that light from the locomotive would be its own undoing in the event of a night attack by enemy aircraft.

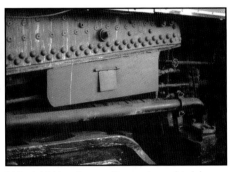

World War II era dispersion shield welded over the left side draft opening of 4449's firebox in 1942 to prevent detection at night by enemy aircraft. Both sides of the firebox received this treatment and the plates were never removed.

## Wartime Austerity and the Daylights

The old question, "What's in a name?" took on unexpected significance to the Southern Pacific during World War II. Its Lima-built 4-8-4s are most often referred to as "Daylights." During the 1940s and 1950s, many of the older enginemen called them "Yellow Jackets." Still others called them "Golden Staters," in reference to their class (GS), which stood for "Golden State." This would soon change.

Because of the great pressure from wartime traffic, Southern Pacific desired to order 16 more GS-4 locomotives from Lima Locomotive Works in 1943. The War Production Board nixed the plan on the grounds that GS-4s were passenger engines and wartime needs called for freight engines.

S.P. then went back, regrouped, and came up with the GS-6 design. The GS-6 engines had smaller 73-1/2-inch-diameter drivers (like the GS-2s), which made them more like a freight engine. And they lacked the streamlined side skirting and colorful red and orange paint of the earlier GS class locomotives. But most importantly, their GS classification was changed from "Golden State" to "General Service." Because it implied freight as well as passenger use, this last item changed the War Production Board's mind and

construction of the 16 locomotives was approved.

Even though the GS-6 design hearkened back to the GS-2, there were some noticeable changes based on operating practice by the S.P. The cabs on the GS-6s were built to the same enclosed design as on the GS-4s and GS-5s.

Someone at Southern Pacific decided in the early 1940s that the Daylights' train indicator number boards would be more easily read at night if they were shifted back to the middle of the boiler, away from the glare of the headlight and oscillating Mars light.

First Southern Pacific Warbaby to arrive on the property was the 4460. It left Lima on July 19, 1943, and posed for this photo at Los Angeles on August 3, 1943. Dispersion shields are already in place. (Gerald M. Best photo)

The GS-6s were among the last Daylights in service as attested to by the 4461 at Sacramento in September of 1956, just a couple months before the fall of steam. (Jim Harrison collection)

All units received this modification, and when the GS-6s arrived from the builder, they came with their lighted train indicators mounted mid-boiler.

This mid-boiler configuration was also adopted on skyline casing-equipped 4-8-2s and 4-6-2s, including the semi-streamlined Pacifics used on the San Joaquin Daylight. Only the stream-lined Sunbeam 4-6-2s of the T&NO (described by David P. Morgan as "Vest Pocket Daylights") kept their train indicators up front beside the smokestack throughout their careers.

At about this same time, neighboring Western Pacific was also feeling the pinch of not enough motive power. So when the W.P. applied to the War Production Board for six engines of the 4-8-4 wheel arrangement, a fateful decision was made.

Time was of the essence. Rather than wait for the builders to tool up for building Western Pacific's design, the Board

*Lima publicity photo of a Western Pacific Warbaby. (Allen County Historical Society collection)*

*Classic Lima builder's photo of the Western Pacific GS. (Kenneth G. Johnsen collection)*

*Three-digit Daylight. Western Pacific's GS number 485 was selected to be the representative of the W.P. GS Class in Lima's builder's photos. Except for the three-digit number, it looks exactly like a Southern Pacific GS-6. The GS Class was called the 481 Class on the Western Pacific. (Allen County Historical Society collection)*

*Lima builder's photo of Western Pacific 485 shows the train indicator boards actually in use. This was not allowed in practice, however, because Southern Pacific owned the patent rights to these and several other appliances and devices. (Allen County Historical Society collection)*

diverted six of the Southern Pacific's GS-6s then under construction to the W.P. The Western Pacific GS or 481 Class had the same streamlined pilot, nose, and skyline casing of Southern Pacific's GS-6s.

There were some slight variations, however. Western Pacific requested (and was allowed) to increase the number of staybolts in the firebox. Conversely, some appurtenances protected by Southern Pacific patents were not incorporated in the W.P. engines. An example is the aforementioned lighted train indicator. Western Pacific GS

The white stripe in this Lima photo is a dead giveaway that this tender is for a Western Pacific 4-8-4. (Allen County Historical Society collection)

Front view of Western Pacific tender at Lima Locomotive Works. (Allen County Historical Society collection)

Lima rear view of the W.P. Warbaby cab showing the drawbars and the back end of the booster engine. (Allen County Historical Society collection)

Lima photo of the fireman's side of a Western Pacific GS. (Allen County Historical Society collection)

Lima photo of the backhead and cab arrangement of a Western Pacific Warbaby. (Allen County Historical Society collection)

Engineer's side of the cab of a Western Pacific Warbaby. Jim Boynton would be right at home! (Allen County Historical Society collection)

The feather and stripe are what differentiate this Western Pacific GS tender from its Southern Pacific counterparts. (Allen County Historical Society collection)

*Lima photo of the details of a Western Pacific GS engine's pilot truck. (Allen County Historical Society collection)*

*Boiler of a Western Pacific 4-8-4. Western Pacific put more staybolts in their fireboxes than any of their Southern Pacific counterparts. (Kenneth G. Johnsen collection)*

class engines were built with the same train indicator housing, but they were not used, and the slots for the train number stencils were filled in with sheet metal.

Shortly after the W.P. GS class was delivered and placed into service, the railroad decided to make a modification that visually set them apart from their Southern Pacific brethren. Elephant-ear type smoke lifters were applied to each of the six engines. The Lima design of the front of the skyline casing had incorporated a smokelifting device, but W.P. felt more updraft was needed.

Lima's production run of the worked-over GS-2 design was not to end with the W.P. and S.P. GS-6s. The Central of Georgia also needed locomotives and the War Production Board found it most expedient to have Lima construct eight more units with the same boiler and running gear as the GS-2s and send them to C. of G. Their cabs were open, they had no streamlining, and their tenders were smaller, but there was no mistaking the GS-2 lineage in Central of Georgia's K Class engines, numbers 451 through 458. Enginemen admired the GS classes, both on Southern Pacific and Western Pacific. It is not surprising that, following

*Western Pacific 481 eases the Exposition Flyer to a stop in Oakland, California, on a hot day in July in 1948. Southern Pacific patent rights prohibited the use of the train number indicator boards that Lima built on all the GS engines. So the W.P. put sheet metal in the openings where the number stencils would have gone. (Jim Harrison collection)*

It's March 25, 1951, and the Western Pacific 483 might be feeling just a bit uneasy because of the FT diesel creeping up behind it. The 483 was retired before it was even 10 years old. (Jim Harrison collection)

their wartime careers, they continued in service well over a decade and were among the very last steam locomotives used prior to dieselization.

## Western Pacific Gets Into the Act

I was privileged to be friends for many years with one of Western Pacific's most well-known steam locomotive engineers, the late James E. Boynton. In the early 1980s, Jim penned the following tribute to the S.P. GS-6 class and the W.P. GS class:

"Southern Pacific's GS-6 engines (4460-4469) were placed in wartime duty in 1943 and reflected the austerity of a nation involved in total war. The drivers came down to a moderate 73 inches and six and one half tons of superfluous metal and machinery were eliminated from the general plan. This was necessitated by wartime restrictions, which limited the use of strategic metals to the prosecution of the war effort.

"Six locomotives built for assignment to the Southern Pacific GS-6 class were transferred to Western Pacific ownership on orders from the Office of Defense Transportation. Traffic flow of military shipments had changed like the tide when Germany surrendered and the machines of war then moved

west. Western Pacific was caught up in a severe power shortage and the movement of trains was contingent upon finding serviceable locomotives.

"If the O.D.T. order for transfer had not been issued, Western Pacific engine number 481 would most certainly have become Southern Pacific number 4464. The other relocated 4-8-4s (482-486 inclusive) would have followed in series and as a consequence the 4-8-4 wheel arrangement was finally incorporated into the Western Pacific steam roster.

"The GS designation persisted on Western Pacific; however, they became General Service locomotives instead of Golden State. They were delivered minus all the Southern Pacific improvements that were covered by their patents. Removed were the special burners, demand-type draft appliances, train indicators, etc. Southern Pacific 4469 was the last of 60 Lima-built 4-8-4s on S.P. that could have represented 66 units if the transfer had not been ordered. But then again, war is hell and the GS engines assumed their vested duties whether they packed the feather or the setting sun on their huge tenders.

"After returning from service in World War II, I had the good fortune to fire and run these huge machines and found them excellent in most respects.

I worked on all the W.P. 481 Class engines, pulling passenger trains between Oakland Pier and Oroville, California, and found many new innovations that were normally foreign to Western Pacific concept.

"For years we had ascertained the temperature of crude oil in the tenders by placing an ungloved hand against the oil compartment. The 481s were much refined in this respect and were equipped with a temperature gauge that indicated fuel temperature. This prevented many boilovers, which formerly caused messes beyond comprehension.

"These GS engines had all-weather (enclosed at rear) cabs and one-level cab decks. No other Western Pacific steam locomotive was equipped with such comfort and they were much appreciated by the engine crews, especially in wintertime. The fireman was supplied with a Worthington feedwater pump (Class SA) and an injector to deliver boiler feed.

"The placement of an injector on the left side was also a departure from established practice on Western Pacific locomotives. The injector on feedwater-heated engines was always installed on the engineer's side of the cab. Placing the 'gun' on the left side of the 4-8-4s no doubt resulted in more efficient boiler service and less maintenance to the firebox, flues, and barrel.

"The engineer's side of the 4-8-4s was equipped with a schedule 8-ET brake valve in pedestal form. This brake valve used on the Daylight locomotives was equipped with a changeover control from automatic air mode to electro-pneumatic control. The big Limas had a speed recorder, but the valve pilot equipment used on their Southern Pacific cousins was deleted because of limits imposed by the O.D.T.

"The backhead was cluttered with the usual gauges and valves, including a marine type suspension throttle, water column, and air type steam whistle control. This last mentioned device really took the individuality out of the engineer's musical talent, each blast of the whistle terminating with mechanical abruptness. No initial or terminating sweetening could be affected and no longer could messages be conveyed to an alert and eager family waiting for a loved one.

"What a thrill it was to ride one of these beauties down through the small valley towns at 75 or 80 mph, the huge steamboat type whistle blasts bouncing back from the farm and produce buildings along the right-of-way, the valve motion a blinding blur, a slight whisper of smoke at the stack, and the needle sitting right up on 250. Water danced from top to bottom in the water glass, the water pump gauge hand pulsating across its face. These were the things that made you know you were really railroading! But we all knew it would not last forever.

"With the advent of the diesel-electric locomotives, the aforementioned pleasures and thrills became nonexistent. After Western Pacific took delivery of their FP-7 diesel passenger engines for California Zephyr service, the GS engines were assigned to freight trains on the 1-percent grades in the Feather River Canyon.

"This job, coupled with other operational difficulties, soon pointed up one of the few bad features of the class: The 4-8-4s were very slippery and really 'rawhided' an engineer and fireman on the run up the slot from Oroville to Portola, California. The 481s couldn't grip the rail on drag freights and while the engine traveled only 119 miles between the two terminals, the drivers must have turned the equivalent of 1,000 miles. This caused unusual rail wear, wear on the drivers, and set up a lot of dynamic augment, damaging the roadbed.

"Careful analysis of the situation did not place the blame on these great locomotives. After all, they were de-signed and built for another class of service and for another railroad. Their purpose and design certainly was not for drag freight service on 1-percent grades under low maintenance programs.

"The last Western Pacific steam engine I worked on was engine 486, bringing her into Oakland, California, for delivery to the scrapper. A bitter moment indeed was when I stepped down from the cab for the last time, commiserating with an old friend in the final moments we would spend together. I knew well her final reward as she moved toward oblivion and forever into the dark shadows of transportation history. I whispered, 'Well done,' bowed my head, and hurried off into the roundhouse to register my rest and 486's number for the last time.

"Steam forever, James E. Boynton."

## After the War's End

Western Pacific's version of the Warbabies met their demise sooner than the Southern Pacific's. By 1953 all were out of service. In January of 1953, GS engines 481, 484, and 485 were sold to the Southern Pacific for salvage. The huge 4-8-4s were towed, minus their tenders, from Stockton to the S.P. shops in Sacramento. Southern Pacific cannibalized the W.P. engines for parts to keep its GS engines going.

The W.P. engines all kept their decorative stripes on their pilots. Southern Pacific had removed the pilot stripes from the Coast Line pool of GS engines, including 4457. Yet in early 1956 the 4457 showed up with a striped pilot, no doubt the recipient of a Western Pacific transplant.

The Southern Pacific GS-6 engines continued in service well into the mid-1950s, running out some of their last miles on the Shasta and San Joaquin routes. The 4462 was involved in a wreck at Chiloquin, Oregon, in

Western Pacific 486 and 483 at the end of their days in Stockton, California. Both were last used in January of 1953 but lingered on the property for several years afterward. Sisters 481, 484, and 485 were sold to the Southern Pacific to be cannibalized for parts for their GS-6 fleet. They were sold minus their tenders. (Jim Harrison photo)

Two unmistakable signs of a Western Pacific GS 4-8-4 are the elephant-ear smoke deflectors at the front and the Western Pacific feather emblem on the tender. The skyline casings already had a smoke-deflecting device, but W.P. elected to add the ears to shoot additional air up the side of the smokestack. (Jim Harrison photo)

1953 and became the first S.P. Daylight engine to be scrapped. The rest of the GS-6s were among the last to go.

World War II had put Southern Pacific's fleet of steam locomotives, including the Daylights, to the supreme test and they pulled through with flying colors. They were still relatively new engines in the 1950s when General Motors' diesels started making serious inroads into the Southern Pacific locomotive roster.

# Western Pacific GS Tender Lives Today

*T*he tender from one of the Western Pacific engines lives on at the Portola Railroad Museum in California. Eugene Vicknair of the Feather River Rail Society provides its history:

Our tender is from W.P. 484. W.P. 481, 484, and 485 were sold to the Southern Pacific in January 1953 without tenders. They were the first 4-8-4s to be sold off. The last was 486 in late 1957. It was also one of the last to run, put aside in January 1953, right when her three sisters were sold.

The tenders were renumbered W.P. 81, 82 (ours), and 83, sequentially. The 81 and 82 were assigned as fuel and water tenders to rotary snowplows 3 and 4, respectively. The 83 is reported to have been scrapped before 1960. The 81 was photographed in 1971 serving with 100-ton crane W.P. MW 28 in 1971 and is reported to have been scrapped in that year.

Rotary 4 was retired in 1965 and scrapped two years later. Tender 82 was assigned to the 28's sister crane W.P. MW 27, also a 100-ton crane, around 1965/66. At some point the 82 was renumbered 27-2 and served as a fuel and water tender for the 27 and her support train. It appears that the crane 27 and tender 27-2 (82) were in use as late as 1979/80. This is not bad when you consider she and the 28 were both built in 1909 for the W.P.! They were originally numbered W.P. 1 and 2.

Tender 27-2 was on the property when the museum was formed and was just left with us. At some point the tender had rolled on her side and to this day one side is very scarred and dented.

In the early days of the museum some of us would crawl into the tender through the water fill cover and enjoy some beers and pizza after hours. That tender certainly qualifies as one of the strangest "crew lounges" ever. It was very rusty inside and we always came out dirty. But I was fascinated at the still-in-place "slosh baffles" in the canteen portion.

*Two views of the tender from Western Pacific 4-8-4 number 484, which is now on display at the Portola Railroad Museum in California*

CHAPTER FOUR

# 4449 AND VARIATIONS ON A THEME

*Freedom Train Daylight. 4449 shows off its red, white, and blue colors on its first test run to Skamania, Washington, on May 8, 1975.*

Color was not a consideration on the original "Daylight Limited" of the 1920s—standard olive green was the dress of the day. When the train was upgraded in 1930 and its name shortened to simply "Daylight," an experiment was tried that cloaked it in one of the most unusual color schemes yet seen on a passenger train.

A lacquered silver paint the railroad called "Pearl Gray" was applied to all of the passenger cars. The idea was to use this opalescent paint to reflect sunlight and thus keep the car interior temperatures lower. The pre-GS class engines that pulled the ghost-colored trains retained the classic locomotive black.

## The Many Dresses Worn by the GS Class

Pearl Gray lasted scarcely one season, being difficult to keep clean and never really catching on with the public. It was back to olive green for the Daylight.

With the ascendancy of Angus McDonald to the Southern Pacific presidency in 1933, the railroad once again moved boldly forward in its thinking about exterior color. McDonald envisioned a new dream train for the Daylight that would be fully streamlined from locomotive to observation car, light in weight, and fit in with the colors of California itself.

Many schemes were drawn up before McDonald in 1936 selected the red, orange, and black colors that became synonymous with the Daylight ever after. McDonald wanted the motive power for the new Daylight to be steam powered and streamlined. So every steam locomotive built to power the Daylight, from the first GS-2 #4410

*Original as-built appearance of the GS-2 Class. Gerald Best snapped this picture of the 4411 on the day it first arrived in Los Angeles, January 12, 1937. (Gerald M. Best photo)*

to the last GS-5 #4459, arrived from the builder in full Daylight color scheme. (The GS-6s were black for reasons related to World War II. See Chapter 3.)

The new equipment for the Daylight operated much as a unit train. The cars' sleek appearance was enhanced by the application of full-width diaphragms to form a continuous flowing look to the train's sides.

The train's colors of high performance Dupont Dulux red and orange were divided into three bands, the largest of which was the lower red band. Across the middle section of the locomotive and train was an orange band which was slightly narrower and placed so that it followed the windows of the passenger cars.

The red top, or letterboard band, was the narrowest of the three and initially carried the name "Southern Pacific Lines" in 4-1/2-inch letters on both the locomotive tender and the passenger cars. The lettering was painted in aluminum bronze paint.

*The 4449 and its tender were painted in the original Daylight color scheme of 1941 for an excursion to Montana in 2004.*

Also painted in aluminum bronze were 3/4-inch stripes between the red and orange bands and at the top and bottom of the color bands as well. Everything else below and above the color bands on the cars was painted black.

A black panel was painted at the front of the tender the same height and location as the lower red stripe. It was intended to blend and aesthetically return the curve of the dark opening under the engine's streamlined skirt.

On the engine and tender, all wheel tires were trimmed in aluminum. The engine's streamlined smokebox front was painted in a high temperature resistant aluminum color. Also in aluminum were the raised decorative bands across the pilot, the edge of the pilot platform, the handrails, and the ladder for the cab. The front number plate trim was aluminum, as were the numerals themselves. The field behind the numbers was red.

The streamlined, bullet-shaped classification lamps mounted near the front of the skyline casing were painted aluminum bronze. Also, the train number indicators had a decorative strip of aluminum bronze on their hind portion.

The air horn protruding out from the front of the skyline casing was originally left polished brass, as was the bell under the pilot platform. In later years they were painted over in aluminum. The rest of the engine and tender, above and below the colors, was solid black.

Variants in paint scheme began showing up during World War II. The Warbaby black paint scheme of the GS-6s of 1943 was also applied to a number of earlier Daylights. The GS-2s became black pretty much as a group. Their pilots, while retaining the horizontal metal stripes, were all black. Their smokeboxes were graphite in color and the only relief was the aluminum smokebox front, punctuated by a black ring around the headlight.

Other GS engines, such as GS-4 4449, also received the somber all black treatment toward the end of the war. Unlike the earlier GS engines, however, most of the GS-4s and GS-5s were painted back into the Daylight red and orange colors again after war's end. One group of these engines comprised the motive power pool for the Coast Daylight and this select stable of engines retained their red and orange colors into the mid 1950s.

In 1946 Southern Pacific changed the way the company's name was lettered on all of its tenders. The small letters spelling "Southern Pacific Lines"

During World War II the Daylight locomotives donned the Warbaby look of all black. After the war ended the GS-4s and GS-5s were repainted into the traditional red and orange scheme, but the GS-2s and GS-3s stayed black, ultimately losing their skirting as well. The 4419 shown here on January 9, 1947, has the new lettering on its tender, but hasn't yet lost its skirting. (Bill Bassler photo)

GS-3 4416 had its first break-in run on November 10, 1937. The engine is seen the way it looked when delivered from Lima, complete with white tires on all wheels. (Gerald M. Best photo)

were replaced with the large letters "Southern Pacific." For the Daylight colored steam locomotives, this meant moving the aluminum colored name down to the middle orange stripe. The large 15-inch letters had a thin 1/8-inch outline of black around them to set them off from the orange.

During the late 1940s, the engines in Daylight dress often had a black ring painted around their Mars light, and sometimes around both the Mars light and the headlight. There did not seem to be a hard-and-fast standard for this

After the war ended and after the delivery of the GS-6 Class, it was safe to be seen in red and orange again. This view of the 4449 on January 30, 1949, shows the famous engine painted back into its classic Daylight scheme with large Southern Pacific lettering on the tender. The pilot stripes are still on. This is the Daylight look at its finest. (Gerald M. Best photo)

arrangement, as attested by contemporary photos, and it may well have been the whim of individual paint shops that determined the face put on these engines. Their pilots still retained the embossed horizontal striping, painted aluminum, however.

By the end of the 1940s, Southern Pacific had embarked on a simplification program to reduce maintenance costs. Appliances under the streamlined skirting were sometimes difficult for the shop crews to reach when servicing. With the exception of the locomotives in the Coast Daylight pool, the GS class locomotives began losing their skirts whenever they went in for shopping.

The 4449 is bringing the Starlight overnight train into Los Angeles in August of 1950. By this time it had lost its pilot stripes as the first of the gradual steps toward simplification of the Daylight scheme. (Bob Clark collection)

Postwar 1946 view of 4449 at Glendale suggests that year as the year the engine was repainted out of Warbaby black and into red and orange Daylight. (Robert B. McNeel photo)

Above: Dirty and smudged, 4449 passes through Corona, New Mexico, on November 13, 1949, pilot stripes still intact. (Kenneth G. Johnsen collection)

For about 10 engines during the years 1948 to 1950, this change meant that the locomotive, denuded of its skirts, was all black from in front of the cab to the pilot. Although the pilot's color was changed to black, the embossed stripes were still painted aluminum. From the cab back (including the tender), the Daylight colors were retained, giving the engine a sort of hybrid appearance somewhere between a GS-4 and a GS-6.

Other Daylight engines losing their skirts went to a plain black scheme, which closely resembled that worn by all other classes of Southern Pacific steam locomotives. The tenders became all black with large white "Southern Pacific" lettering on the sides, similar to their non-streamlined brethren. The locomotives likewise were all black with white numerals and lettering on the sides of the cabs.

The smokebox front of these engines, like that of all other S.P. steam power, was painted aluminum. The pilots, unlike on other S.P. steam engines, were also painted aluminum. And there were some variations; with some engines having the entire pilot painted aluminum while others had only the central portion in aluminum. The number plates had aluminum rims and numerals on a

*A few of the GS-4s wore this unusual scheme around 1950. The 4438 is shown in Tucumcari, New Mexico, in May of that year. The skirting has been removed, the pilot is black with silver striping, and the cab and tender retain their red and orange colors. (Arnold Menke collection)*

*At Taylor shops in Los Angeles, the 4447 is receiving a lot of attention from the shop crew on April 16, 1950. It has been hypothesized that the hybrid paint scheme applied to some of the GS-4s in 1950 was used to make them more similar in appearance to the 4-8-2 Mountain locomotives, which had Daylight colors on their cabs and tenders. The two were often paired on the helper district for the San Joaquin Daylight. (Frank Peterson photo from the collection of Alan Miller)*

*Because Southern Pacific wanted to convince the War Production Board that the Daylights were "general service" locomotives, they were all given a coat of somber black paint to make them look like other steam engines. The GS Classification was changed from "Golden State" to "General Service." 4449 kept its Warbaby scheme a year or so after war's end and is shown here at Alhambra on November 7, 1946. (Bill Bassler photo)*

black field. Bullet-shaped classification lamps continued to be aluminum in color.

The Coast Daylight pool of engines kept their Daylight red and orange colors until the dieselization of that train in January of 1955. But simplification was employed here, too. The metal stripes on the pilot were removed and the pilot became solid orange. Field behind the numbers on the front number plate became simple black at this time.

The Daylight logo at the front end of the skirt had long been a time-consuming job to paint by hand. Daylight locomotives that retained their Daylight paint scheme into the 1950s did not keep their logos when repaint time came.

## 4449 Wore All the Standard Paint Schemes

GS-4 number 4449 holds the distinction of having worn more color

*It's December 20, 1953, and the Coast Daylight is departing Los Angeles for San Francisco. The look is still all red and orange Daylight. (Bob Slocum photo)*

schemes than any other Daylight, by virtue of its having been the only skirted one preserved. Fresh from Lima in 1941, the 4449 was dressed as all other Daylights of the era: full red and orange with Daylight emblems on its flanks and small "Southern Pa-

cific Lines" across the top stripe of its tender.

In response to evolving needs during World War II, 4449 carried first the dispersion shields over all of its lights, and later the all-black paint scheme employed by the railroad to convince

*Some might argue that a logo like this on a tender was way ahead of its time, but the railroad ended up changing only the size and location of the lettering on tenders. And the "lines" was dropped in 1946. (David Joslyn photo from the collection of Gerald M. Best)*

The story of one unusual paint scheme is included here even though it was never adopted by the railroad. Gerald Best, a Warner Brothers Pictures executive, was an avid S.P. fan and photographer in the 1930s and 1940s. He had taken a good photo of the first GS-6 to arrive on the property in Warbaby paint in 1943.

Southern Pacific's photographer forgot to take a photo of it, and so Jerry gave S.P. one of his negatives in exchange for a pass to visit S.P. yards throughout the war and take engine pictures. He became friends with S.P. company photographer Dave Joslyn and they frequently traded negatives.

One day a GS-6 had its picture taken with a medallion on its tender instead of "Southern Pacific Lines." Here is its story in Jerry's own words:

For a long time this story was a secret between Dave Joslyn and me. The 4468 had just come out of the shop, newly painted and polished, and Joslyn as the company photographer was sent down to photograph it. He took the old 8 x 10 camera that he had used for so many years, set it up and took several shots for the company.

Then the paint foreman remarked that a freight car emblem stencil he had would look better than the words "Southern Pacific," so Dave said why not try it. So the painter sprayed black over the conventional lettering, the stencil was sent for, and Dave shot a couple of 8 x 10s of it.

Then he did what he always did on a fine setup; he used a film holder that had two slides, each 4 x 10. He would back away from his 8 x 10 location until he had a good postcard image on the lower 4 x 10 section, shoot one picture, replace the slide, and refocus on the upper 4 x 10 section. This produced a second postcard negative when cut down to 4 x 6, and one went to me.

In this case, after Dave had developed the negatives, and the paint foreman had sprayed out the circular emblem and relettered the tender, he got cold feet and came up to Dave's office and asked him if he would mind destroying the negatives, as he was afraid of the reaction from the front office if they didn't like it.

So Dave gave him the still-wet 8 x 10s and the foreman cut them into little pieces. But he didn't know about the postcard shots. So when Dave sent the negative down to me, he asked me not to circulate any prints from the negative until after he had retired from the S.P.

I kept my promise, but of course when Dave died and his collection was sold to Guy Dunscomb and myself, Guy got the other postcard shot. That medallion was on the tender less than five minutes.

*The clandestine paint scheme was tried on the 4468 and quickly removed. Photographic evidence shows that this paint scheme was also tried on the 4467 at a different time. It was never adopted. (David Joslyn photo from the collection of Gerald M. Best)*

the War Production Board that the engine was a dual purpose locomotive.

With the end of the war and the return to peacetime, the Daylights, including 4449, blossomed forth in their Daylight colors once more. The 4449 at this time carried the large "Southern Pacific" lettering on its tender's orange stripe in place of the original "Southern Pacific Lines" on the upper red stripe.

The only Daylight color scheme the 4449 did not wear was the black engine, skirtless ahead of the cab, with red and orange still splashed across the cab and tender in the traditional way. The 4449 was one of the engines included in the Coast Daylight pool of steam locomotives, and thus kept its full Daylight regalia until the early part of 1955.

The 4449's look in July 1953 at San Francisco. (Jim Harrison collection)

By the time the end came for Daylight red and orange in 1955, 4449's dress had been simplified to the solid orange pilot, black field behind the front numbers, and lack of Daylight emblems on its flanks. After its last general shopping in March of that year, 4449 was black and skirtless like its other GS-4 sisters.

The 4449 finished its first active career on the Southern Pacific on September 24, 1956, dressed in the basic black of all Southern Pacific steam locomotives. It remained this way for the next year and a half, wiling away the months in storage at Bakersfield. When its new lease on life (as Portland's display locomotive) came

Nearing the end of its days, the 4454 presents a bleak, weary appearance that is a stark contrast to the days in 1942 when it posed for builder's photos at Lima as the representative of the second group of GS-4s. It is June 30, 1956, and the former beauty queen is at Mission Bay, running out its last miles on commuter trains. (Jim Harrison collection)

The look of the San Joaquin Daylight in her last days of steam. On September 14, 1956, just nine days after this photo was made at Berkeley, diesels would take over number 51 and 52. (Jim Harrison collection)

Boxpok main drivers were replaced on a few GS engines with disc drivers as seen on the 4437 on August 21, 1954. (Arnold Menke collection)

The 4449 as it looked when it was placed into Portland's Oaks Park Transportation Museum in 1958. Black hinges, white tires, and white running boards are not exactly the way the engine looked during its service life on the S.P. (Walt Grande photo)

A slight variation in paint schemes is seen on Southern Pacific's last Daylight, number 4469, on March 24, 1956. The pilot silver treatment is carried all the way across the pilot beam and steps. And the bullet-shaped classification lamps have been painted black instead of silver. (Fred Stindt photo)

After losing its skirts and colors in 1955, the 4449 spent its final year of service on Southern Pacific in the simple black scheme of all the Daylights in their final days. (Wilbur Whittaker photo)

driver wheels. The hinges of the smokebox front were painted black, as were the rims around the headlight and Mars light. Grabirons on the front of the smokebox were black and the air horn was painted silver. Lettering remained standard.

## The Most Colorful Daylight of All

Over the next 16-1/2 years, the custodians of the 4449 at Oaks Park in Portland occasionally painted the engine, and gradually returned it to the basic black scheme of its final days of service on the S.P. Its next scheme, however, would be the most radical ever worn by a Daylight.

The American Freedom Train Foundation, conceived by Ross Rowland, was making plans to run a red, white, and blue train throughout the United States in 1975–'76 as part of the nation's bicentennial celebration. This train would carry the artifacts of our nation's history and heritage to the far reaches of America for one and all to see.

There was never any question from the beginning—A.F.T. would be pulled by a steam locomotive. Actually three steam locomotives as it turned out, but that story is for the next chapter. Selection of Daylight 4449 to be the

in 1958, the shop crews at Bakersfield gave it a fresh coat of paint, replaced some broken glass, and sent it on its way to the Rose City.

From this point forward, the 4449 was to wear some unique dresses never dreamed of by the people back at Lima in the 1930s. The first was applied in April 1958, after it arrived at Portland's

Brooklyn roundhouse. Someone there decided it needed some sprucing up before it went into the park on display.

The engine emerging from Brooklyn shops that April did not look like the Daylights in anyone's memory. There was white striping on the running boards along the boiler as well as on the rims of the pilot wheels and principal locomotive for the Freedom Train set into motion a search for the right color scheme that was not unlike the original search in 1936.

The walls of the roundhouse office in Portland, site of the 4449's restoration for the Freedom Train, were covered with hastily taped-up drawings of a GS-4 engine and tender with a variety of red, white, and blue color schemes. The merits of each were debated for days and input from Foundation headquarters back east was also considered.

The scheme that finally evolved was a logical extension of the white cars of the train itself. Painted white were the tender body, the cab, and the upper stripe along the boiler (which had originally been red in the Daylight scheme).

At the bottom of the sides and back end of the tender a red over blue stripe, carried forward from the cars, ran horizontally and then abruptly angled up to the level of the bottom of the cab. This upturn coincided with the black panel at the front of the tender simulating the end of the opening under the engine's streamlined skirting.

The red and blue striping continued on the locomotive's skirt, dropping down to include the pilot. The long ago removed metal stripes on the pilot were not reinstalled, but instead were simulated in white paint. Smokebox front remained silver colored and the rest of the locomotive and tender remained black except for the pilot and driver wheels, which were trimmed in white. The number boards were brought forward on the skyline casing to simulate the original Daylight look.

Pepsi-Cola had been one of the original million dollar sponsors of the Freedom Train. The soft drink giant kept the Freedom Train crew car #1776 stocked with its product at all times. Because of this sponsorship and because of its red, white, and blue colors,

*Southern Railway green and Freedom Train red, white, and blue don't exactly mix, but who cares? They make a splendid sight crossing the bridge at Clemson, South Carolina, on August 28, 1976. (Bob Clark photo)*

*Freedom Train Daylight. 4449 shows off its red, white, and blue colors on its first test run to Skamania, Washington, on May 8, 1975.*

some insiders referred to the train as the Pepsi-Cola Train.

The Freedom Train finished its run in Florida at the end of 1976 and locomotive 4449 was slated to go back home to Portland. But before it did, Southern Railway invited the curious looking streamlined 4-8-4 to make a series of steam-powered excursions on its lines through the South. The 4449 made an interesting contrast, in its patriotic colors, to the drab cars of the Southern Steam Excursion program.

On its Amtrak-sponsored return trip to Portland in the Spring of 1977, the 4449 wore its Freedom Train colors with the addition of large "Amtrak" letters applied to the tender in the lower red/blue stripes. Seeing the world's first Amtrak steam Daylight did not seem to faze people who were already used to seeing a red, white, and blue GS-4s.

Hibernation in Portland for the next few years following 1977 did not see any changes to 4449's paint scheme. 1981 would change all that! The State of California was planning a grand opening for its state-of-the-art railroad museum in Sacramento in the spring of 1981. A splashy railfair was to be held, invitations to which were sent to operational steam locomotives all over the globe.

The 4449's invitation to Sacramento was precisely the impetus needed to get it painted back into authentic Daylight colors. 4449 engineer Doyle McCormack, by now an employee of the Southern Pacific, obtained S.P.'s permission to run the Daylight to California and even got the railroad to pay for repainting the engine and tender.

Imron, a type of liquid plastic "paint" undreamed of at Lima in the early days, was used to bring the 4449 back to Daylight appearance and keep

An Amtrak Daylight? Seeing is believing; Amtrak sponsored the 4449's return trip home to Portland, and so its name was emblazoned across the Daylight's tender. Photo is near Dorris, California, on April 30, 1977.

Looking just like Lima Locomotive Works in 1941, S.P.'s yard in Portland is site of the unveiling of "the most beautiful train in the world" on April 4, 1981. The Daylight logo isn't painted on yet, but the gleaming red and orange GS-4 looks like it is ready to couple onto 98 and head for Los Angeles. California State Railroad Museum's grand opening Railfair '81 was the impetus that got 4449 back into correct dress.

it that way for a long time. The red and orange and black GS-4 that backed out of its stall in Portland's Brooklyn Roundhouse for the first time on April 4, 1981, looked ready to couple onto the Coast Daylight of, say, 1949 and speed it on its way.

Large "Southern Pacific" was emblazoned across the orange stripe of the tender, the number boards were moved back to mid-skyline casing, and the pilot had its stripes (although at this time still only painted on in a grayish-white color). Like any new technology, the Imron paint had been difficult to apply. But the gleaming result that basked in the warm spring sun that afternoon was well worth the effort it had taken.

The Sacramento Railfair trip was a smashing success, which popular-ized the Daylight to new generations who had never seen an original red, orange, and black Daylight. Soon plans were being drawn up for a bigger, more ambitious trip—the 1984 New Orleans World's Fair Daylight. For this huge undertaking, sponsored in part by Trail-ways Bus tycoon Roger Peck, the 4449 received a major overhaul. New flues were installed, new driver tires were

Time to get serious about keeping 4449 roadworthy. New tires, new flues, new bearings, and a host of other improvements were made to the 4449 in preparation for its major trip to the New Orleans World Fair in 1984.

Except for the diesel, the clock is turned back 30 years as 4449 races toward Sacramento on April 26, 1981.

In its colorful dress, Daylight 4449 was the undisputed star of Railfair '81. (Leon Callaway photo)

New tires cast in England were sweated on to 4449's wheels in 1984. (Terry Parker photo)

*Recreating the look of the Daylight in California as 4449 and the World's Fair Daylight pass Niles Tower on May 8, 1984.*

cast overseas, shipped to Portland, and sweated onto the wheels, and a complete 13-car train of matched Daylight colored cars was assembled.

Beginning with the New Orleans outing, over the next 20 years, the 4449 underwent numerous changes in paint schemes, some very radical and others very slight. They are discussed chronologically through the rest of this chapter so that the Daylight modeler, student, and historian can identify the different looks possessed by the 4449 at different times in its second active career as a Daylight.

The appearance differences that distinguish the World's Fair Daylight from the California Railfair Daylight before it were a lack of white trim on the pilot wheels and driver wheels and (finally) metal decorative stripes added to the pilot. The decorative stripes on the pilot were made of stainless steel instead of the original ordinary steel to simplify painting (by eliminating the need to paint the stripes aluminum).

A red, orange, and black canteen car was fabricated from a surplus cab-forward 4-8-8-2 tender by removing the oil compartment to allow the entire car to carry water. The top of the tender was streamlined to blend with the train (although it was considerably wider) and the canteen became 4449's companion on its longer journeys.

Stainless steel stripes notwithstanding, the World's Fair Daylight with its 13 matched Daylight cars came as close to capturing the look of the original Daylight as anything yet seen outside

*Looking not unlike the Coast Daylight of the 1940s, 4449 and the 1984 Louisiana World's Fair Daylight have left San Francisco and are headed for the San Joaquin Valley line. Making the look even more authentic is the fact that 4449's canteen car developed a hotbox in San Jose and had to be left behind for repairs.*

*With the numerals "52" in the number boards and an authentic consist strung out behind its tender, 4449 looks every bit the San Joaquin Daylight of yore. But it's 1984!*

*Doyle McCormack calls the World's Fair Daylight separation incident at Del Rio, Texas, "the worst day of my life." The retaining plate that holds the pin in place in the drawbars somehow broke, allowing the pin to drop out and the engine to separate from the tender and train on the run. But in a masterful display of ingenuity and perseverance, Doyle and crew found the lost pin, fixed the broken plate, fashioned new tender hoses from donated fire hoses, and had the train up and running again in a little over three hours. Sometimes worst days turn into shining moments. (Terry Parker photo)*

*The World's Fair Daylight returns home past a classic Southern Pacific photo site; Northern California's Mt. Shasta. (Tim Repp photo)*

In 1987 Portland held a railfair and the 4449 made its appearance wearing black paint on the outer rim of its Mars light. It kept this same scheme the following year when it pulled the Spirit of the West special for Philip Anschutz, the president of the Rio Grande railroad, which had just purchased the Southern Pacific. Using former California Zephyr equipment and the Southern Pacific business car fleet, Anschutz toured his new empire behind steam.

Centennial Winter Games in Wenatchee, Washington, in 1989 saw the Daylight heading up a special train in the snow still wearing the 1987 dress. But by May of that year, 4449 was headed to Los Angeles for the 50th anniversary of Los Angeles

of model railroads. And although the trip was not a financial success, anyone who saw the train or rode on it will certainly never forget it.

The 4449's next outing came in 1986 when Touchstone Pictures hired it to star in a movie along with Burt Lancaster and Kirk Douglas entitled *Tough Guys*. The script called for the Daylight, alias the "Gold Coast Flyer," to be commandeered by Lancaster and Douglas and run at high speed into Mexico for their getaway. The visible changes to the 4449 during shooting were a "Gold Coast Flyer" emblem in place of the Daylight emblem and a fake pilot for scenes involving a collision with an automobile. A remarkably accurate full-sized wooden mockup of the Daylight and the front part of its tender were constructed for the movie's wreck finale.

*The 4449 became a Rio Grande Daylight when the Denver & Rio Grande Western bought the Southern Pacific. President Phil Anschutz came to see his new empire and posed with the crew of his special train, "The Spirit of the West."*

The 4449 was invited to the 50th anniversary of the opening of the Los Angeles Union Passenger Terminal in 1989 and reprised the appearance of the 4426 fifty years earlier. (Leon Callaway photo)

Both Union Pacific's 4-8-4 number 8444 and Southern Pacific's 4449 were invited to the Los Angeles Union Passenger Terminal's 50th anniversary, and both engines passed through Cajon Pass at the same time resulting in the inevitable race. We won't mention who won, but the U.P. engine had diesel helpers! (Leon Callaway photo)

Union Passenger Terminal with its Mars light and its headlight rimmed in black.

1989 was a busy year for the 4449. In September it had another movie role, this time in *Come See The Paradise*, a film about Japanese people being sent to internment camps. The 4449's skirts were removed and a temporary siding affixed to the side of the front steps. The headlight and Mars light retained their black rings, joined by the lighted number boards of the smokebox front. Then the entire engine and tender were coated with a water-soluble soot gray paint to give the engine an in-service look, much the way a model railroader would weather his trains. Some of the red and orange coloring barely showed through, but not the Southern Pacific lettering.

By November 1989 the soot paint was washed off, the lights all had aluminum colored rims, and the engine looked pristine for its run to Yakima, Washington's Steamfest. For a brief time in 1990 the State of Washington required the Daylight to have a yellow flasher on its nose, perched above the Mars light. This requirement was removed by the time of the 1990 Yakima Steamfest, to which the Daylight again journeyed dressed as before.

The 10-year anniversary of the California State Railroad Museum in 1991 gave 4449 its next outing and there was a slight change in appearance: The "Southern Pacific" lettering on the tender was painted more correctly than it had been during the steamfest.

The next year 4449 again went to California, this time to San Jose where it teamed up with Pacific 2472, and its one little change in appearance was a black field behind the numbers on the front number plate.

In 1996 the 4449 made a round trip to Vancouver, B.C. By the following year on its trip up to Wishram in the Columbia River Gorge, the field on the number plate was once again red. Its appearance stayed the same for the 1998 trips to Wishram and Bend, Oregon.

As the 4449 enters Selah Gap on one of its Washington State trips, it is greeted by one of Yakima's famous trolleys.

Daylight 4449 meets restored Pacific 2472 at Sacramento's 10th anniversary Railfair in 1991. Railfan & Railroad editor Jim Boyd set up a classic night shot.

Fifty years separate the faces of passenger motive power in this view of the Amtrak Coast Starlight passing the Daylight returning from a trip through Washington State. (Tim Repp photo)

## A Daylight Like No Other Daylight

The year 2000 saw two radical changes in 4449's appearance. Burlington Northern Santa Fe rented the 4449 from the City of Portland to use on a series of "Employee Appreciation Specials." For these trips the engine, tender, and canteen were painted entirely black with thin white stripes delineating where the orange band would have been on the skirt and tender sides. The pilot and driver wheels were trimmed in white and the numbers on the cab and tender were white. The number plate field as well as the builder plate field was painted red. B.N.S.F. emblems were affixed to the center of the sides of the tender and canteen and to the locomotive skirt about where the Daylight logo would have been.

Following the B.N.S.F. specials, the Southern Pacific Historical and Technical Society held their convention in

In 2000 and 2001 the Burlington Northern Santa Fe passed up its own native locomotives (SP&S 700 and AT&SF 3751) and hired Doyle McCormack and the 4449 to pull its Employee Appreciation Specials around the country. The 4449 got a look not even the Western Pacific Daylights could equal.

In response to the terrorist attacks of 9/11, Doyle decided to paint the 4449 back into Freedom Train colors. The canteen car is black and bears the inscription, "Let's Roll" as the train passes over the high bridge at Madras, Oregon.

Portland and requested the 4449 to be in steam. The engine was to be used again the next year by the B.N.S.F. in the black scheme, so Doyle McCormack (in order to avoid two massive repaintings) surprised the S.P. group with an all black "Warbaby" Daylight. The 4449 had small "Southern Pacific Lines" at the top of the tender as in 1943, dispersion shields over the lights, Mars and number light frames black, builder and number plate fields red, and wheels solid black. Side white striping was covered over with black tape.

In 2001 it was back to work for the Burlington Northern Santa Fe again. This time there were no emblems on the skirt or tender and the "Southern Pacific Lines" remained. The white stripes were restored but the wheels remained black. Builder and number plates had red fields and both the headlight and Mars light had black rims.

In 2002 a Deschutes River trip to Bend, Oregon, was made. Partly in response to the terrorist attacks of 9/11

and partly to let a new generation see it, Doyle decided to paint the 4449 back into Freedom Train colors. Observable differences from the first Freedom Train scheme were the stainless steel stripes on the pilot and the red field on the builder's plate. The canteen car remained black and was emblazoned with the words "Let's Roll."

The Montana Daylight, operated over the Montana Rail Link in 2004, saw the 4449 come full circle in color schemes. It was basically restored to its 1941 appearance of red, orange, and black color scheme, with small "Southern Pacific Lines" lettering at the top of the tender, and a correctly proportioned number board on the skyline casing near the front. Aside from some of the latter day appliances in the cab, the only two giveaways that this engine is not some kind of time traveler from 1941 are the red field on the builder's plate and the stainless steel stripes on the pilot. The folks that built the 4449 at Lima would be proud of their creation's appearance 65 years later.

In 2004 the 4449 came full circle in appearance when it once again wore the color scheme it was given at Lima Locomotive Works in 1941, some 63 years before.

## CHAPTER FIVE

# END OF THE LINE AND THE SURVIVORS

*Daylight body parts. The overturned top of a GS tender, the amputated cab from number 4440, and other rubble will soon be melted down as the majority of the Daylight fleet meets its end. (Roy E. Shepherd photo)*

Dieselization of America's railroads, while generally agreed to be inevitable, actually came quicker than most people expected. Rapid fulfillment of diesel locomotive orders in the 1950s, coupled with a slump in business in the last half of that decade, hastened the demise of steam.

With the exception of the early-bird Western Pacific, the Class 1 railroads in the West dieselized within the two-year period from 1957 to 1959. It had been anticipated that steam would be around until sometime after 1960, but expected harvest rushes in the falls of those final years of the '50s did not materialize, and the railroads were able to proceed with full dieselization.

## Daylight Finale and the Alamo of Southern Pacific Steam

Coast Daylights 98 and 99 were the first Daylight trains to exchange steam power for diesel (if you don't count the Shasta Daylight which began its career diesel powered in 1949). Deliveries of EMD E-9 passenger diesels and Alco PA units completed through 1954 allowed Southern Pacific to announce dieselization of its Coast Line passenger fleet. D-day was set for January 7, 1955.

Roller bearing-equipped 4458 pulled #98 to Los Angeles and sister 4459 pulled #94, the Starlight (itself soon to be a casualty to passenger train consolidation), on their final steam powered runs. Three unit EMD and Alco diesels were now in charge, and could pull the passenger trains over the Cuesta grade out of San Luis Obispo without helpers.

Following D-day there still were a couple dozen Daylight steam engines

The victor. After January 7, 1955, Coast Line passenger trains were pulled by diesels like this Alco PA. (Kenneth G. Johnsen collection)

serving in the Coast and Los Angeles pools. Many made their way north to what became the Alamo of Southern Pacific steam: the commute runs on the peninsula between San Jose and

The vanquished. Classic, full-skirted Daylight steam locomotives powered the Coast Daylight until the beginning of 1955 and then were relegated to their last stand on the commuter runs between San Francisco and San Jose. (Kenneth G. Johnsen collection)

San Francisco. As steam was winding down in other districts, the 4-6-2s and 4-8-2s of the commute pool were becoming supplemented and supplanted with GS engines. All were painted the workday black of S.P. steam power.

Following January 7, 1955, it was not too unusual or surprising to see a bright red and orange Daylight at the head of a drab commute run bound for San Jose. This was not to last, however. Within the first few months of 1955, the last holdouts lost their skirts and colors and settled in to what would be their final days of service for Southern Pacific. And a vigorous service it was!

Many commute trains were run each way at rush hours, their tight schedules demanded that the trains stop quickly at each station, discharge their passengers in minutes, and sometimes seconds, and march right out of town as fast as they could accelerate. The Daylight locomotives, with their speedy 80-inch drivers, were up to the challenge.

Although diesels were tried beginning in 1953, steam power pulled the commuters through the end of 1956. I remember riding the dieselized Coast Daylight from San Francisco to

---

A GS-2 or GS-3 bursts out of the fog at Bayshore going 65 miles per hour just weeks before the final steam-powered commuter run. (Arthur Hamilton photo)

The fog lifted on this December 1956 afternoon, rewarding Art Hamilton with this stirring action shot of GS-4 4444 rounding the big curve at 7th Street in San Francisco. (Arthur Hamilton photo)

The 4432 was scrapped at Los Angeles in September of 1956. The end is never pretty. (Arnold Menke collection)

When one considers the load already borne by the main pin when pulling a heavy train, it is hard to imagine a force strong enough to shear it completely off as happened to this GS-2 in 1940. (Robert B. McNeel photo)

Glendale in the spring of 1956 as a 10-year-old. With my nose pressed to the glass, I watched with excitement as GS after GS moved commuters into San Francisco while my sleek streamliner moved out.

The end of exciting railroading came, however, on January 22, 1957, when a GS-4, #4430, pulled the last steam-powered commuter—and as such, S.P.'s last regularly scheduled steam-powered passenger train—into history. Train Number 146 left San Francisco at 5:45 PM bound for San Jose. When the lanky Daylight was uncoupled and drifted to the roundhouse after its run, nearly a century of steam-powered passenger railroading on the Southern Pacific came to an end.

Long rows of retired steam engines accumulated at S.P. engine terminals in 1957 and 1958. GS-5 4458 is seen in one of them at Oakland on June 26, 1957. During their careers, steam engines often swapped tenders at shoppings. It is interesting to see that this roller bearing-equipped GS-5 has somewhere along the line acquired a friction bearing-equipped tender from a GS-4. (Leon Callaway collection)

# Was Steam Intentionally Done In?

Much has been written about conspiracies to eliminate the steam locomotive from America's railroads. Steam's proponents will say General Motors sold their diesels to the railroads at below cost to get them to switch. Diesels' proponents say that steam was too labor intensive and too costly to keep operational.

By 1950 the major steam builders had built their last steam locomotives and it was clear the diesel had the upper hand. The flashy new units were attractive to operating departments and the incentive was to make them look favorable to management. Did they sometimes run up large expenses on steam locomotive maintenance to make them look bad? Consider the case of the GS-6 #4465.

The 4465 received major work and then was run out to the dead line. (Kenneth G. Johnsen collection)

Review of the 4465's *Annual Inspection and Repair Report* dated November 8, 1956, reveals it received new flues, staybolts, and fusible plugs on that date, scarcely two months before the final regular steam operation on the Southern Pacific. Following the shopping on November 8, the engine was run light the 18 miles to Roseville, placed in the dead line, and never turned a wheel again. This same scenario is known to have happened to many S.P. steam engines. Was it done intentionally to run up steam locomotive maintenance costs or just poor timing? You be the judge.

*Inspection report for the 4465 showing the major work done to it at this late date. (Richard Lohse collection)*

The 4430 remained on the roster until September of 1958. A number of the Daylights were kept under steam for several days after January 22 and then placed into storage at places like Bayshore, awaiting possible future needs by the railroad. The arrival of more diesels and a drop in business squashed that possibility forever.

Some excursions were run in 1957 and 1958 behind steam power. GS-4 4443 thrilled fans on a March 1957 outing and then played a supporting role in the Frank Sinatra movie *Pal Joey.*

One can conjecture whether it was Sinatra's love for trains (he was a big Lionel collector) that led the producers to use a tired, but still beautiful, Daylight in the movie, or whether steam power was just cheaper to rent in 1957 than diesel power. Nevertheless, the movie opens with a nostalgic scene of the 4443 rolling to a stop at the Oakland Mole to the sweet strains of Nelson Riddle's orchestra playing "Bewitched, Bothered and Bewildered."

GS-6 4460 pulled several excursions in those years and headed the final official S.P. steam trip, a two-day excursion from Oakland to Reno and back, October 18-19, 1958.

*After the fall of steam, several fantrips were run using GS engines. The 4443 was still serviceable in 1957, so it powered this special in Niles Canyon on March 24th. (Tom Gildersleeve photo)*

*Deep within the bowels of the Oakland Mole, S.P. 4443 is learning what it's like to be an actor. Opening scenes of Frank Sinatra's movie* Pal Joey *have the 4443 rolling to a stop and Sinatra getting off the train and walking past the one-time Daylight. Filming was done in April of 1957. (Jim Harrison collection)*

The 4460 smokes it up for the photographers on a photo run-by on the final Southern Pacific steam trip in October of 1958. (Arthur Hamilton photo)

## San Joaquin—the Last Steam-Powered Daylight

The San Joaquin Daylights #51 and 52 had continued to run behind steam after the Coast Daylight was dieselized in January 1955. Some of the GS class from the coast, including final tripper 4458, had found their way to the San Joaquin Valley in 1956. Steam at the time was still in frequent use for freight

The old and the new. Hard working GS-4 4441 is helping a freight over Altamont Pass on October 7, 1956. The soon-to-be retired steam engine is sandwiched between a mechanical refrigerator car and a bay window caboose. Signs of changes to come... (Tom Gildersleeve photo)

up and down the valley, in addition to pulling the San Joaquin Daylight between Oakland and Bakersfield. (Diesels—normally a 4-unit F-7 A-B-B-A lashup—took over the train at Bakersfield and marched it up Tehachapi and over its loop to Los Angeles.)

During these final months of steampowered Daylights, an unusual element in the consist made the San Joaquin Daylight unique among the world's steam-powered passenger trains: dome cars.

The San Joaquin Daylight had been the recipient of many hand-me-downs in passenger equipment in the past. As Noon Daylight and Coast Daylight consists were upgraded and

Train time at Bakersfield. The diesels that brought the San Joaquin in from Los Angeles have been cut off and the 4449 has coupled on and is marching 51 out of town on its way to Oakland. (Andy Saez photo from the collection of Tom King)

GS-6 4465 in freight service. As more and more GS engines were bumped by diesels from passenger service, they wound up in freight service on districts still using steam. (Kenneth G. Johnsen collection)

It is November 27, 1955, and tired GS-4 number 4435 is pulling freight assignments more and more now. In less than a year it was retired and sold for scrap to Luria Brothers in South San Francisco; not a very fitting end for a streamlined passenger locomotive that was once the finest thing on rails. (John Hungerford photo from the collection of Tom Moungovan)

Imagine riding in a full-length dome car behind a hard-working 4-8-4. This delight was possible during the final year of steam operation on the San Joaquin Daylight. (Jim Harrison photo)

renewed, their older equipment was transferred to #51 and 52. But in 1954 Southern Pacific began building full-length dome cars in their shops. The first of these went into service on the San Joaquin Daylight and for a little over a year in the mid-1950s it was possible to ride in the air-conditioned splendor of a full-length dome car behind a hard-working Daylight 4-8-4 steam locomotive.

In the San Joaquin Valley, as elsewhere, the same basic scenario was being played out between steam and

Bakersfield was a hub of steam activity in 1955 and 1956. The San Joaquin Daylight was still steam powered north of here and there was plenty of steam freight action. The 4428 is waiting on a ready track for the diesel-powered Daylight to arrive so that it can speed it on its way to Oakland. (Tom King photo)

It's October of 1954 and the Railway & Locomotive Historical Society has sponsored a fantrip using two GS-4s; the 4447 and the 4449. The 4447 has already gotten the black treatment, but the 4449 is among the last holdouts in the Coast Line passenger pool to still be dressed in Daylight finery. It displays its good looks at the photo stop at Humphries, California, unaware that within six months it too will be all black. (Bob Slocum photo)

The 4443 was one of three Daylights that were used for fantrip service in 1957. It is seen here crossing the Kern River with a fan special. (Stanley Snook photo from the collection of Jim Harrison)

GS-6 4460 is pulling the "Fresno Flyer" fantrip in October of 1958. (Arthur Hamilton photo)

Run-by for the fans is performed by the 4439 at Goshen Junction in March of 1957. (Arthur Hamilton photo)

GS-4 4439 was one of the active fantrip engines in 1957, seen here speeding south in the San Joaquin Valley. (Kenneth G. Johnsen collection)

diesel. Fulfillment of new locomotive orders was occurring just as a slump in traffic hit the railroads. Steam locomotives' days were numbered. After September 14, 1956, diesels pulled the San Joaquin Daylights.

GS-4 4449 had lost its skirts along with its red and orange livery in March of 1955. The now black and silver Daylight was transferred from the Coast Line power pool to the San Joaquin Valley where it spent its final days in both freight and passenger service, truly justifying its General Service designation.

The 4449's fires were killed for what turned out to be the last time on

The 4449 rests in the dead line at Bakersfield on July 13, 1957. Vandals have broken all glass and birds are roosting in its skyline casing. The future for this latter-day celebrity was not looking very bright at this point in its career. (Herman Friedrich photo)

September 24, 1956. Traffic slowdowns were the reason it had not been called back into service as expected that fall. On February 21, 1957, Southern Pacific assigned the 4449 to a group of steam engines designated "stored serviceable" and placed it in a long line of similar locomotives at Bakersfield.

Even though the S.P. obligingly ran a number of fan trips behind steam in 1957 and 1958, the 4449 was not one of the locomotives used to power them, nor was it called to duty on a few unscheduled, non-excursion steam operations during the last three years of the 1950s. Excursion engines included the 4439, 4443, and the 4460.

## Preserved Daylights

Southern Pacific was one of the more generous railroads when it came to donating steam locomotives for display in parks and fairgrounds during steam's waning years. Any town along S.P.'s route could request a locomotive and have it delivered by the railroad ready for display. The town needed only provide a suitable final resting place and the means to move the engine there from the S.P. tracks.

Because they were small and easier to move about, 16 S.P. 0-6-0s found their way into city parks in the late 1950s. Larger, more cumbersome

In the spring of 1958, what was to be the last non-fantrip movement of a Daylight locomotive under steam on the Southern Pacific took place. Richard Lohse, son and grandson of career S.P. men, remembers the bittersweet event:

The stationary steam plant at Sacramento would shut down every spring for its annual inspection. The 4455 was placed on house steam at the Roseville roundhouse on April 2, 1958. On April 3 she was fired up. An inspection was performed which included the testing of the dynamo, injector,

water pump, air pumps, and brakes. At 8:40 PM she was run light to Sacramento and placed in the roundhouse where she provided stationary steam for three days. By April 7 her fire was stilled and the last use of a GS Daylight engine in non-fantrip service had ended.

*The 4455 was pulled off the dead line and given an inspection to assure its roadworthiness for its three-day stint as a stationary boiler. (Richard Lohse collection)*

*Back side of inspection report reveals that when the 4455 was called for the last unscheduled operation of a Daylight locomotive in April of 1958, it had been out of service since September of 1956. (Richard Lohse collection)*

*Former beauty queen, down on her luck, having literally her last gasp. The 4455 presents a truly pathetic appearance on its very last duty as a substitute for the roundhouse boiler at Sacramento. Look at the scuffs and dirt, the bent handrail, the numerals missing from its number plate, and its overall tired look. The end will come in a couple days. (Richard Lohse photo)*

engines were usually passed over. As a result, only three 4-6-2s survived. On the T&NO a handful of Mikados and a 2-10-2 made it into parks while out in California one 4-10-2 was given to the Los Angeles County Fairgrounds at Pomona. One 4-8-2 in Oregon almost survived, but at the last minute in 1961 it was scrapped after all. The last cab-forward 4-8-8-2 and the C.P. Hunting-

ton were retained by S.P. for display outside the station in Sacramento.

Two GS Daylight locomotives were donated by S.P. for preservation. The first was the 4449 stored at Bakersfield. The City of Portland, Oregon, requested a large engine for a transportation display it was setting up on a narrow strip of a park along the Willamette River. The S.P. responded by

pulling the 4449 out of the Bakersfield storage line, cosmetically refurbishing it, and hauling it dead in train to Portland in April of 1958.

The Oaks Park Transportation Museum lies immediately adjacent to the Portland Traction Company's tracks. A temporary switch placed in the P.T. line, along with about 100 yards of track leading down into the

S.P. 4449's Cinderella story began in 1958 when it was selected to be preserved at Portland, Oregon. The Daylight was moved from Bakersfield to Portland in April of that year, where it was spruced up for display. (Walt Grande photo)

Sacramento paint shops on April 15, 1959. Why is a steam locomotive being freshly painted by the railroad at this late date, months after the last steam run? The engine is the 4460 and it has been donated to the National Museum of Transport in St. Louis. S.P. wanted it to look fresh for its final trip east. (Ted Wurm photo)

display site, made it easy to move the huge Daylight 4449 into its "final" resting place. Here it joined Spokane Portland & Seattle 4-8-4 #700, Union Pacific 4-6-2 #3203, Finnish State Railway 2-8-0 #418, and Stimson Mill 2-truck Shay #1.

GS-6 4460, although damaged in a sideswipe accident in November of 1956, remained active into 1958 with several "farewell to steam" excursions. The last of these, on October 18-19, was the last official steam operation on the Southern Pacific. (See S.P.H.&T. S. S.P. *Trainline* #83 for an interesting article on other non-official S.P. steam operations into 1959 and 1960.)

Following its final run, the 4460 was spruced up by the railroad and dispatched to St. Louis, Missouri, to be placed in the National Museum of Transport. Unlike its glamorous GS-4 sister, Warbaby 4460 has sat exposed to the elements, a motionless museum piece, for nearly half a century.

For 16 years it seemed GS-4 4449 would also be relegated to the dismal life of a static display engine. Birds in Oaks Park nested in its skyline casing. A thief stole its builder's plates. Vandals broke its headlight and Mars light. A couple of runaway girls lived for a time in its cab. Portland's 40+ inches of rainfall each year accelerated the massive engine's rust.

There was a bright spot to 4449's existence. A young man named Jack Holst occasionally visited Oaks Park to view the steam engines he loved. He kept 4449's lubricator reservoirs filled with oil. Each time he visited the park, he would turn the lubricator's crank, keeping oil on the bearings and axles. Like many of us, he dreamed of someday seeing the 4449 come back to life, and this was his own way of contributing to that possibility.

And what a contribution it was! Had he not kept the bearings and axles from corroding and freezing up, the cost to replace them later would have been in the hundreds of thousands of dollars, making the 4449 not a suitable candidate for restoration. Alas, Jack Holst died a young man and did not live to see his dream come true.

## American Freedom Train Daylight

The American Freedom Train of 1975–'76, conceived by Ross Rowland and financed by contributions of $1 million each from Pepsico, Prudential Insurance, Kraft Foods, and General Motors, provided 4449 with a ticket out of Oaks Park. The locomotive search team for the Freedom Train narrowed their candidates down to three 4-8-4

The 4449 wiling away the years at Oaks Park Transportation Museum in Portland on September 5, 1965, unaware of the dramatic turn of events that lies in store for it.

# Restoring the 4449 for the American Freedom Train

*Doyle McCormack, the 4449's engineer and the Chief Mechanical Officer for the American Freedom Train, remembers the process of bringing 4449 back to life for the Freedom Train's Bicentennial tour.*

"You big S.O.B.!" That was my first impression of the 4449. I just stood there in Oaks Park looking up at her. As I walked around her I thought, "Oh God." It was a new experience for me; I had never been exposed to anything quite that big-looking before. I had worked with Nickel

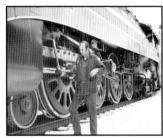

*Doyle McCormack and his steed the 4449 in the Blue Mountains of Oregon on October 25, 1975.*

Plate Berkshire 759 and Grand Trunk Western 4070 with their little 69- and 70-inch drivers and now I was looking at this 80-inch drivered monster and all I could think of was how huge it was.

We selected the 4449 to pull the American Freedom Train mainly by process of elimination. We were looking for a general overall engine that could go 90 percent of the places we had to go. The criteria included being oil-fired, being big enough to pull the train, being an engine of modern design, and being available.

Various engines around the country were considered. We narrowed our list down to half a dozen or so and made inspections of these candidates. Union Pacific 8444 is a good engine, but the Union Pacific said they wouldn't let it off their system. Santa Fe 2925 was another, but its physical size (with that great big tender behind it) cut down the list of cities we would have been able to visit. Nickel Plate 763 was in better condition than the 4449, but it was coal fired, and in order to make it oil fired we would have had to make too many changes.

If you compare a Nickel Plate Berkshire to a Southern Pacific Daylight, it's like comparing a Chevrolet to a Cadillac. Both were fine machines in their own class. You could sense similarities in design because they were both Limas. The Nickel Plate 700s were basically a 50-mile-an-hour freight engine, designed for 4,500 tons of freight, whereas the Daylights were 80-mile-an-hour passenger engines. So when we looked them all over, the Daylight, because of its design and availability, was really the best candidate.

Looking back on 4449's restoration, I was crazy as hell to ever start on it. But experience is a good teacher, and after the Freedom Train, there is very little now that scares me in the way of mechanical projects.

We found a few surprises on her that were not apparent on our first inspection. The crown sheet had a crack in it; I didn't expect the superheater units to be as bad as they were; and there were a few other things like that, which kind of slowed us down. And then some political problems also lost us a couple weeks.

The project was made a little more difficult because of the time element. I had to sacrifice money in a lot of instances for the sake of time. It could have been done a little cheaper, but I had to buy time.

Our projected time frame was 90 days, and it took us 129 days from

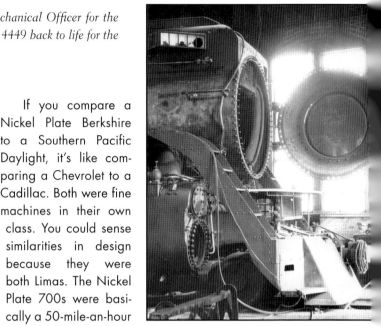

*In a view very reminiscent of 1941 Lima erection hall scenes, the 4449 is being taken apart and restored in earnest for its job pulling the American Freedom Train. Photo is at the former Spokane, Portland & Seattle (S.P.&S.) roundhouse in Portland on February 23, 1975.*

*Lagging is being applied to the 4449's boiler. At one time the plan was to renumber the engine "1776" and the number board in this photo reflects the idea. Fortunately wiser heads prevailed and the 4449 kept its original Daylight number. (Doyle McCormack photo)*

moving her into the roundhouse on December 14, 1974, to first fire-up on April 21, 1975. I wouldn't hesitate a minute to do the whole project again. But I would like to have one of those projects someday where I didn't have a deadline; just do it at my own pace.

On the road 4449 was the kind of engine that an engineer dreams about. Being around her for two years made me appreciate her more and more every day. The longer I was around her the more attached I got to her.

You look at the Daylights and you have to think, "Where did the people go that put this thing together and where did they get their ideas?" There was so much design in it, that you wonder where that type of ingenuity is today. There isn't a part on that engine that wasn't made to be worked on. When you can take a locomotive of more than 400 tons and make it relatively simple to work on, you have to ponder, "What happened to that line of thinking?"

The 4449 represents, as far as I'm concerned, the epitome of design for an American steam locomotive, and probably had more effect on my life than any other single event. If it weren't for the 4449, I'd still be sitting back in Conneaut, Ohio, fat, dumb, and happy in my ignorance. She broadened my horizons (and those of my wife Laurie) and gave us the opportunity to see what the rest of the world is really like.

The 4449 has a future as long as it can get Class 1 railroad cooperation. Somebody has to let you run the thing. As I say, there is no mechanical project that scares me, and I can assemble the people to make it run and run right whenever the word comes down, "Yes, we can do it."

After sitting in Oaks Park for over 16 years, the 4449's fortunes are about to be changed. An advance inspection crew from the American Freedom Train Foundation has come to inspect the Daylight for possible use on the Freedom Train. The verdict: definitely restorable! (Kenneth G. Johnsen collection)

type locomotives: Union Pacific's 8444 based in Cheyenne, Wyoming, Santa Fe's 2925 stored in Belen, New Mexico, and Southern Pacific's 4449 resting in Portland, Oregon. Even though the Union Pacific and Santa Fe engines were newer and in better mechanical condition, the A.F.T. team selected the 4449.

The 4449 was thought to have more charisma than the other engines. The term "most beautiful train in the world" has been applied to the Daylights so often that even a fair portion of the lay public can recognize them. Once a preliminary inspection in 1974 deemed it restorable, the selection team lobbied heavily for the 4449. They got their wish, and Doyle McCormack was appointed chief mechanical officer to oversee its restoration thanks to his experience restoring a Nickel Plate Berkshire.

The 4449 was carefully removed from Oaks Park on December 14, 1974, and towed on its own wheels across town where it was deposited into Burlington Northern's Hoyt Street (former S.P.&S.) roundhouse for restoration. Work began immediately and was carried on almost 'round the clock by a small paid staff of skilled workers and a large group of volunteers—including myself—who carried out the "grunt" work. Slightly more than four months later, on April 21, 1975, the Daylight was fired up and moved under its own power for the first time in 19 years.

*Continued on page 93*

Volunteers on the Freedom Train project took various subassemblies to restore at home. The newly refurbished number board is one such project.

Moving day, December 14, 1974, finds the 4449 carefully inching its way around the tight curve before crossing the Willamette River. The moving crew literally walked with the engine the whole way from Oaks Park to the Hoyt Street roundhouse in order to keep all parts lubricated. (Kenneth G. Johnsen collection)

The paint was literally still wet on 4449's pilot as it spun around the turntable in celebration of its successful restoration on April 21, 1975.

Ed Immell and crew are installing the 4449's bell just shortly before the engine made its first movement under steam on April 21, 1975.

The 4449's boiler is ready for lagging. Wheels and tires are looking good in fresh paint.

Triumphant moment! The 4449 rolls out of the roundhouse for the first time under its own power in over 17 years. The restoration is a success.

With skirting completed and Freedom Train colors freshly applied, the 4449 ventures out on its first test run. The outing has taken it across the Columbia River to run on the former Spokane, Portland & Seattle line in Washington State.

May 16, 1975, will be a busy day for the 4449. All road tests have been completed and it's time to be off to pick up the Freedom Train. But first there will be a christening ceremony with the Portland Rose Queen and her court as she breaks a bottle of champagne across the Daylight's pilot. Then there is a short trip over to Swan Island to be on public display with a Union Pacific Centennial. The 4449 is starting to feel what it's like to be a celebrity.

During part of the American Freedom Train's tour, a Reading junkyard queen, 4-8-4 Number 2101, was hastily put into operating condition and hauled the train around some of its eastern venues. It's seen here with the train full of artifacts at Archbold, Ohio, on June 13, 1975. (Bob Clark photo)

Texans had to put their own spin on things and pulled Texas & Pacific 2-10-4 Number 610 out of display in Fort Worth and restored it to operation for the Texas portion of the Freedom Train's run. Photo is at Bryan, Texas, on February 18, 1976. (Allen Rider photo)

Changing of the guard. The handsome 4449 meets its smaller eastern counterpart at the Pentagon in Arlington, Virginia. (Arnold Menke photo)

Restoration was finished in May and a couple of test runs were made, demonstrating the engine's roadworthiness. In June the red, white, and blue Daylight left Portland for the East Coast to join the Freedom Train already underway.

Eastern promoters of the Freedom Train wanted an engine of their own to pull it and hastily refurbished former Reading junkyard queen #2101. This engine pulled the Freedom Train throughout much of the Northeast, not, according to Doyle McCormack, because of any size restrictions as is often reported, but because of the particular preferences and twisted politics of some eastern members of the A.F.T. team.

Similarly, in the state of Texas people want to do things their own way. Museum piece Texas & Pacific 2-10-4 #610 was removed from display and refurbished for service. The big Texas type pulled the Freedom Train on its tour through the Lone Star State and then went back into hibernation.

The 4449 took over the Freedom Train in July and marched it around the country for 11 months before relinquishing it back to the 2101 for approximately four months. In September 1976 the 4449 took over once again and guided the train through the completion of its tour in Florida on December 31, 1976.

By any measure the Freedom Train was a huge undertaking and a public relations success. Almost seven million people toured its exhibits and several times that number saw it from trackside. The train covered 24,612 track miles and visited 138 cities in the lower 48 states.

For aficionados of Southern Pacific Daylights, however, the lasting benefit of the Freedom Train was the restoration of the 4449 to operating condition. With the big 4-8-4 renewed and having five years of flue time, the Freedom Train provided the turning point in 4449's career that would keep it a living, breathing steam locomotive rather than a rusted park relic.

Following the Freedom Train stint and some excursions in the South on the Southern Railway, the 4449 headed home in 1977 and awaited a somewhat

Continued on page 98

For its Christmas, 1975, visit at Pomona, California, the Daylight became Santa Claus. (Dave Edwards photo)

Doyle McCormack tends the feedwater heater at Sarasota, Florida, on December 7, 1976. (Bob Clark photo)

The Freedom Train is crossing the Blue Mountains of Oregon on October 25, 1975, as seen from 4449's cab. Union Pacific provided the 26-car train with a helper for this portion of the ascent.

Some of the Freedom Train's travel was done at night like an old-fashioned circus train, moving from one day's stand to the next, scarcely allowing a moment's relaxation. Tom Gildersleeve made this spectacular night photo of the 4449 and Freedom Train passing through Oil Junction, California. (Tom Gildersleeve photo)

As the amply powered Freedom Train roars through Tehachapi, California, a California Highway Patrolman, lights flashing and sirens screaming, tries vainly to get the motorcade to stop. He may as well wait until they get to the next stop at Pomona. (Leon Callaway photo)

Two modern movies have used the 4449, bringing it even more fame. *Tough Guys* (1986) with Burt Lancaster and Kirk Douglas featured the locomotive as the "Gold Coast Flyer" (painted on its skirt in the same script and location as its "Daylight" logo). The plot had Lancaster and Douglas as elderly train robbers who wanted to pull one last job. They hijacked the 4449 from its engineer (played by Doyle McCormack himself) and ran it into the desert, climaxing with a dramatic train wreck running off the end of the track into the dirt. The studio utilized a live steam model and a full-sized wooden mockup of the 4449's boiler, cab, and part of its tender for the effect.

Another scene had the 4449 crashing into a car as a police SWAT team tried to close in on the criminals. A fake pilot was constructed and applied to the 4449's own pilot so that the original would not be harmed in the collision. Daylight cars from Portland were used for the 4449's train.

*Come See the Paradise* (1990) with Dennis Quaid and Tamlyn Tomita utilized the 4449 as the locomotive for a train moving displaced Japanese Americans to internment centers. Although the on-screen appearance of the 4449 in this movie was fairly brief, the engine was filmed in and about the Portland, Oregon, depot for over three days.

A remarkably accurate full-sized wooden mockup of the 4449 was built for the grand climax of the movie Tough Guys. The script called for the engine to half bury itself in the sand when it ran off the end of its track, something they couldn't do with the real thing! (George Lavacot photo)

A fake pilot covering the real one allowed 4449 to slam into the stalled car in the movie Tough Guys without sustaining damage. (George Lavacot photo)

To look the part of a grimy wartime engine, the producers had McCormack and crew remove the 4449's side skirting. A wash of water-soluble grime was sprayed over the entire engine and tender almost obliterating its red and orange coloring. The look was not unlike that of the final steam years on the S.P. The producers had consulted me to find out what the Daylight should look like during the World War II era. I urged them to use dispersion shields and paint the locomotive black, but that didn't fit with their idea of a standard steam engine in the old days and so the ideas were not used. For the train itself a set of vintage coaches from Canada was rented and lettered for Southern Pacific.

*No skirts and lots of dirt gave the producers of* Come See the Paradise *the look they wanted for a World War II vintage steam powered train to haul Japanese citizens to internment camps. Three days of filming produced only a few minutes on screen for the Daylight.*

*Chuffing about Portland's station for the movie* Come See the Paradise, *4449 and the old heavyweight passenger cars conjure a scene from many years ago. But it's really September 18, 1989.*

uncertain future. Uncertainty ended in the spring of 1981 when promoters of the California State Railroad Museum helped bring the 4449 to their grand opening "Railfair '81" celebration—wearing true Daylight livery!

From that point on, Daylight 4449's continued existence as an excursion engine seemed assured. Many consider it to be the most popular locomotive in America. (Oh alright, it's not Thomas the Tank Engine, but of the real live locomotives on America's railways today, none have been seen by more people than S.P. 4449.)

In addition to roles in movies, the 4449 has visited Canada, hauled a world-class recreation of the entire Daylight train from Portland to New Orleans and back, and helped with numerous celebrations such as Los Angeles Union Passenger Terminal's 50th anniversary, California State Railroad Museum's 10th anniversary, and on and on. Even Burlington Northern Santa Fe hired Doyle McCormack and the 4449 to power "Employee Appreciation Specials," painted in a one-of-a-kind black B.N.S.F. paint scheme, passing over its own "native" engines S.P.&S. 700 and Santa Fe 3751, which were operable.

## Wrecks and Scrapping

Getting back to the fate of the other GS engines, Western Pacific's Daylights were the first to be retired. In 1953 Western Pacific sold three of their GS engines to Southern Pacific for use as spare parts sources. Engines 481, 484, and 485 were towed, minus their tenders, from Western Pacific's shops in Sacramento across town to Southern Pacific's shops. Parts off of them, such as the still-embossed ribbed pilots, were soon observed on S.P. engines still operating past 1953. Western Pacific retained the tenders for their own use with derricks and snowplow trains.

*With her brief reprieve as a fantrip engine over, the black-eyed 4439 is now on her way to the scrap yard of National Metals at Los Angeles. (Leon Callaway photo)*

*Daylight body parts. The overturned top of a GS tender, the amputated cab from number 4440, and other rubble will soon be melted down as the majority of the Daylight fleet meets its end. (Roy E. Shepherd photo)*

The first Daylight on S.P. to be retired and scrapped was Warbaby 4462, involved in a bad rollover accident at Chiloquin, Oregon, in July of 1953. Three more were retired in 1954, seven in 1955, twenty in 1956, seven in 1957, and the remainder in 1958. The last one to actually meet the scrapper's torch was the 4444 in August of 1959.

The 4444 did leave a slight legacy, however. Its tender was converted into a "hammer car" for testing impacts on freight cars with hydracushion frames.

cars, as well as too short a stopping distance between block signals.

Another spectacular wreck was a head-on collision at Redlands, California, on February 11, 1945. The 4443 was pulling out of town with the Californian when her engineer failed to observe a yellow block signal. Three-cylinder 4-10-2 number 5015 was preparing to pull into a siding to allow the passenger train to pass, when the Daylight engine smashed head-on into it at about 40 miles per hour. Both engines were rebuilt for continued service.

Even a Western Pacific Daylight engine was involved in a dramatic wreck, a prominent scar that it

*Rollover wreck of the 4462 at Chiloquin, Oregon, on July 25, 1953, gave the GS-6 the dubious honor of being the first Daylight to be scrapped. (Kenneth G. Johnsen collection)*

*Only a few months old and 4446 looks like it's ready for the junk heap. The rear-ending of the Lark on September 19, 1941, inflicted heavy damage to the front of the Daylight, but it was rebuilt and put back into service. (John Hogan collection)*

Bayshore shops rebuilt it in 1960–'61 and its tests were carried out for the next 11 years. It was scrapped, however, in 1972.

Several Daylights were involved in serious accidents over the years. Unlike the 4462, however, they were rebuilt for continued service. An early one involved the 4446 when it was still only a few months old. Train Number 76, the Lark, had made an unscheduled stop for a stalled automobile at Wellsona, California, on September 19, 1941. The 4446 was propelling the Fast Merchandise Freight number 374 behind it and was unable to stop in time to avoid smashing into the rear end of the Lark. Forty-eight people were injured. Subsequent investigation blamed lack of high-speed brakes on the freight train's

The Daylight's engineer didn't notice the block signal was against him as he pulled out of Redlands, California, with the 4443. A 4-10-2 was attempting to get out of his way, but there was no time to avoid the collision. (Redlands Daily Facts)

*Wreck of the Exposition Flyer at Pilot, Nevada, resulted in Western Pacific's first fatalities. The train was routed through a 10-mile-an-hour switch, but the W.P. 482's engineer didn't know it was coming. (Jim Boynton collection)*

carried for the rest of its life. Number 482 was speeding W.P.'s crack Exposition Flyer through Pilot, Nevada, on April 5, 1946. A section crew was working on the main line and had set a 10-mph switch to detour all trains around the work. The 482's engineer either didn't know about or forgot about the detour and his train left the rails as it flew through the switch. Seventy-six people were injured and two were killed, the first fatalities on Western Pacific. The punched-in smokebox front had to be replaced, but the streamlined rounded Lima type wasn't available, so a flat version was applied, giving this engine a distinct appearance from then on.

Other Daylight mishaps included a rollover of the 4430 in the Arizona desert in 1952, a wreck involving 4445 and 4471 in 1954, a sideswipe of the 4460 at Davis, California, in 1956, and a head-on between a GS-4 and a 4-8-0 at Salinas at an unknown date.

Except for the 4449 and 4460, all other Daylights suffered ignominious ends at the hands of scrappers' torches in industrial areas like South San Francisco, Terminal Island, and even the S.P. shops at Sacramento. A few builder's plates, number plates, classification lamps, etc., made their way into collectors' hands, but other

Details are sketchy, but this collision between a Daylight and 12-wheeler 2923 is believed to have occurred at Salinas sometime in the late 1940s or early 1950s. (Lee Thwaits collection)

The 4430 seems to have sustained more damage from the wrecking cranes than from its rollover accident in the Arizona desert in 1952. (Al Augenstein collection)

than these, the photographic records and a couple sound recordings are all we have with which to remember the rest of the great Daylight GS-2 through GS-6 locomotives.

## Southern Pacific GS-Class Locomotives Built By Lima

Disposal Notes

1. Sold for scrap to National Metals at Los Angeles.
2. Scrapped at Sacramento.
3. Sold for scrap to Purdy Company at South San Francisco.
4. Sold for scrap to Purdy Company at Los Angeles.
5. Scrapped at Los Angeles.
6. Sold for scrap to Luria Brothers at Los Angeles.
7. Sold for scrap to Luria Brothers at South San Francisco.
8. Sold for scrap to California Metals.
9. Donated to the City of Portland, Oregon.
10. Donated to the National Museum of Transport, St. Louis, Missouri.
11. Sold for scrap to Luria Brothers at Richmond.

| Locomotive Number | Construction Number | Road Class | Date Built | Setup Date* | Retirement Date | Disposal Date | Disposal Notes |
|---|---|---|---|---|---|---|---|
| 4410 | 7646 | GS-2 | 12-36 | 1-14-37 | 5-14-56 | 6-6-56 | 1 |
| 4411 | 7647 | GS-2 | 12-36 | 1-15-37 | 2-8-56 | 4-20-56 | 2 |
| 4412 | 7648 | GS-2 | 12-36 | 1-16-37 | 12-3-56 | 12-21-56 | 2 |
| 4413 | 7649 | GS-2 | 12-36 | 1-16-37 | 2-8-55 | 5-16-55 | 6 |
| 4414 | 7650 | GS-2 | 12-36 | 1-21-37 | 11-24-54 | 1-14-55 | 2 |
| 4415 | 7651 | GS-2 | 12-36 | 1-26-37 | 2-17-58 | 11-3-58 | 3 |
| 4416 | 7721 | GS-3 | 10-37 | 11-3-37 | 4-5-55 | 6-1-55 | 6 |
| 4417 | 7722 | GS-3 | 10-37 | 11-9-37 | 8-13-56 | 10-29-56 | 2 |
| 4418 | 7723 | GS-3 | 10-37 | 11-9-37 | 12-10-57 | 12-12-58 | 4 |
| 4419 | 7724 | GS-3 | 10-37 | 11-16-37 | 5-25-55 | 7-20-55 | 6 |
| 4420 | 7725 | GS-3 | 10-37 | 11-16-37 | 5-21-58 | 5-7-59 | 1 |
| 4421 | 7726 | GS-3 | 11-37 | 11-23-37 | 9-24-58 | 5-7-59 | 1 |
| 4422 | 7727 | GS-3 | 11-37 | 11-26-37 | 11-29-57 | 5-20-59 | 4 |
| 4423 | 7728 | GS-3 | 11-37 | 12-1-37 | 12-28-54 | 1-21-55 | 2 |
| 4424 | 7729 | GS-3 | 11-37 | 12-7-37 | 9-19-55 | 11-4-55 | 2 |
| 4425 | 7730 | GS-3 | 11-37 | 12-7-37 | 5-14-56 | 7-13-56 | 5 |
| 4426 | 7731 | GS-3 | 11-37 | 12-18-37 | 6-12-56 | 7-18-56 | 11 |
| 4427 | 7732 | GS-3 | 12-37 | 12-21-37 | 2-8-55 | 2-25-55 | 1 |
| 4428 | 7733 | GS-3 | 12-37 | 12-29-37 | 9-24-58 | 4-24-59 | 1 |
| 4429 | 7734 | GS-3 | 12-37 | 12-30-37 | 2-8-55 | 4-7-55 | 2 |
| 4430 | 7798 | GS-4 | 3-41 | 4-11-41 | 9-24-58 | 7-13-59 | 7 |
| 4431 | 7799 | GS-4 | 3-41 | 4-15-41 | 9-24-58 | 3-25-59 | 8 |
| 4432 | 7800 | GS-4 | 4-41 | 4-28-41 | 5-14-56 | 9-14-56 | 5 |
| 4433 | 7801 | GS-4 | 4-41 | 4-19-41 | 10-5-56 | 11-15-56 | 3 |
| 4434 | 7802 | GS-4 | 4-41 | 4-19-41 | 5-14-56 | 10-12-56 | 5 |
| 4435 | 7803 | GS-4 | 4-41 | 4-26-41 | 10-18-56 | 12-13-56 | 7 |
| 4436 | 7804 | GS-4 | 4-41 | 4-28-41 | 5-2-57 | 7-1-57 | 8 |
| 4437 | 7805 | GS-4 | 4-41 | 4-29-41 | 9-24-58 | 7-17-59 | 1 |
| 4438 | 7806 | GS-4 | 4-41 | 5-1-41 | 12-26-56 | 2-7-57 | 2 |
| 4439 | 7807 | GS-4 | 4-41 | 5-3-41 | 5-21-58 | 3-23-59 | 1 |

| Locomotive Number | Construction Number | Road Class | Date Built | Setup Date* | Retirement Date | Disposal Date | Disposal Notes |
|---|---|---|---|---|---|---|---|
| 4440 | 7808 | GS-4 | 4-41 | 5-6-41 | 9-27-56 | 10-31-56 | 11 |
| 4441 | 7809 | GS-4 | 4-41 | 5-6-41 | 9-24-58 | 7-17-59 | 1 |
| 4442 | 7810 | GS-4 | 4-41 | 5-10-41 | 5-14-56 | 5-31-56 | 1 |
| 4443 | 7811 | GS-4 | 4-41 | 5-15-41 | 9-24-58 | 10-31-58 | 8 |
| 4444 | 7812 | GS-4 | 4-41 | 5-18-41 | 9-24-58 | 8-7-59 | 3 |
| 4445 | 7813 | GS-4 | 5-41 | 5-21-41 | 9-24-58 | 3-23-59 | 1 |
| 4446 | 7814 | GS-4 | 5-41 | 5-21-41 | 9-24-58 | 11-3-58 | 3 |
| 4447 | 7815 | GS-4 | 5-41 | 5-27-41 | 5-14-56 | 6-6-56 | 1 |
| 4448 | 7816 | GS-4 | 5-41 | 5-27-41 | 12-26-56 | 1-24-57 | 7 |
| 4449 | 7817 | GS-4 | 5-41 | 5-30-41 | 10-2-57 | 4-24-58 | 9 |
| 4450 | 7848 | GS-4 | 3-42 | 3-27-42 | 9-24-58 | 10-29-58 | 4 |
| 4451 | 7849 | GS-4 | 3-42 | 3-31-42 | 9-24-58 | 3-25-59 | 4 |
| 4452 | 7850 | GS-4 | 3-42 | 4-4-42 | 10-18-56 | 11-7-56 | 11 |
| 4453 | 7851 | GS-4 | 3-42 | 4-4-42 | 2-7-57 | 3-14-57 | 7 |
| 4454 | 7852 | GS-4 | 3-42 | 4-14-42 | 5-2-57 | 8-7-57 | 7 |
| 4455 | 7853 | GS-4 | 4-42 | 5-4-42 | 9-24-58 | 3-23-59 | 1 |
| 4456 | 7854 | GS-4 | 4-42 | 5-6-42 | 12-26-56 | 2-8-57 | 7 |
| 4457 | 7855 | GS-4 | 4-42 | 5-9-42 | 6-12-56 | 7-18-56 | 11 |
| 4458 | 7856 | GS-5 | 6-42 | 6-21-42 | 5-21-58 | 10-31-58 | 8 |
| 4459 | 7857 | GS-5 | 5-42 | 6-5-42 | 12-26-56 | 1-25-57 | 8 |
| 4460 | 8013 | GS-6 | 7-43 | 7-31-43 | 10-31-58 | 4-16-59 | 10 |
| 4461 | 8014 | GS-6 | 7-43 | 7-31-43 | 5-21-58 | 3-25-59 | 8 |
| 4462 | 8015 | GS-6 | 7-43 | 8-11-43 | 1-15-54 | 3-5-54 | 2 |
| 4463 | 8016 | GS-6 | 8-43 | 8-14-43 | 6-12-56 | 7-17-56 | 11 |
| 4464 | 8248 | GS-6 | 8-43 | 8-21-43 | 5-21-58 | 10-21-58 | 4 |
| 4465 | 8249 | GS-6 | 8-43 | 8-27-43 | 9-24-58 | 3-23-59 | 4 |
| 4466 | 8250 | GS-6 | 8-43 | 8-30-43 | 12-28-54 | 6-14-55 | 5 |
| 4467 | 8251 | GS-6 | 8-43 | 8-31-43 | 4-5-55 | 5-13-55 | 2 |
| 4468 | 8252 | GS-6 | 8-43 | 9-7-43 | 2-7-57 | 3-8-58 | 7 |
| 4469 | 8253 | GS-6 | 8-43 | 9-7-43 | 9-24-58 | 4-24-59 | 1 |

*Engines 4410 through 4415 were set up at Los Angeles; 4416 through 4469 were set up at El Paso.

## Western Pacific 481-Class Locomotives Built By Lima

Disposal Notes

1. Sold to Southern Pacific Company at Sacramento, less tenders.
2. Sold for scrap to Hyman-Michaels Company at San Francisco.
3. Sold for scrap to Purdy Company at South San Francisco.

| Locomotive Number | Construction Number | Road Class | Date Built | Setup Date | Last Used | Disposal Date | Disposal Notes |
|---|---|---|---|---|---|---|---|
| 481 | 8017 | 481 | 6-43 | 7-14-43 | 12-51 | 1-53 | 1 |
| 482 | 8018 | 481 | 6-43 | 7-19-43 | 1-52 | 2-53 | 2 |
| 483 | 8019 | 481 | 7-43 | 7-20-43 | 1-53 | 1-56 | 3 |
| 484 | 8020 | 481 | 7-43 | 7-30-43 | 3-52 | 1-53 | 1 |
| 485 | 8021 | 481 | 7-43 | 7-31-43 | 10-51 | 1-53 | 1 |
| 486 | 8022 | 481 | 7-43 | 8-4-43 | 1-53 | 9-57 | 3 |

*The 4445 and the 4471 collided in 1954 with these results. Even at this late date the 4445 was rebuilt for continued service. Note the temporarily applied footboards to the Daylight's pilot beam. (Al Augenstein collection)*

# CHAPTER SIX

# APPRECIATING THE MOST BEAUTIFUL TRAIN IN THE WORLD

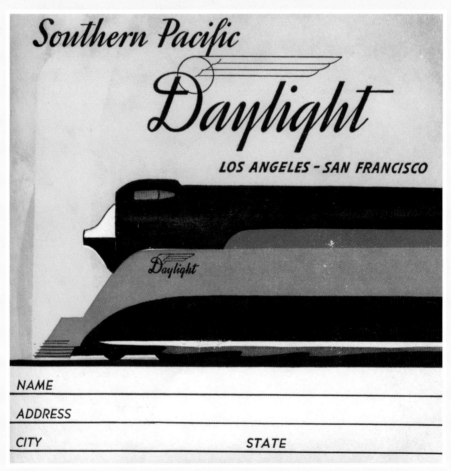

Baggage sticker distributed for use on the Daylight. (Kenneth G. Johnsen collection)

On board the Daylight train was a person who brought around a cart or a tray, which had candy, snacks, and souvenirs for sale. These items might include playing cards with a color painting of a Daylight racing past Santa Barbara's mission, postcards of the train or the scenery it passed through, picture books, a striped "Southern Pacific Junior Engineer" cap with logo, or a kid's whistle shaped like a generic steam locomotive (not the Daylight). My brother still cherishes his "Southern Pacific Junior Engineer" cap, a memento of a trip on the Coast Daylight half a century ago.

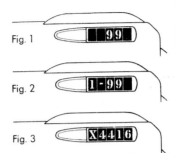

## WHAT THE NUMBERS ON OUR LOCOMOTIVES MEAN

On either side of the boiler near the smoke stack or further back, indicators are displayed. These are "train numbers" (See figure 1).

All trains going *toward* San Francisco are called "westward" trains and are odd-numbered such as 1, 3, 5, and so on. All trains going *away* from San Francisco are called "eastward" and are even-numbered such as 2, 4, 6, and so on. A train going north from San Francisco is an "eastward" train, while a train going north from Los Angeles is a "westward" train because it is going to San Francisco. Figure 1, for example, shows 99 as the train number which is the number of the streamlined *Daylight*, northbound.

In order to carry all the people wishing to ride on the same train, it is sometimes necessary to operate the train in two or more separate parts, which are called "sections." When a train is operated in sections, the first section carries a "1" preceding the train number as shown in figure 2. The second section carries a "2" preceding the train number, etc., and the last section carries the train number only. Special trains or "extras" carry the locomotive number preceded by an "X" (See figure 3).

Fig. 1 ⬛ 99
Fig. 2 1-99
Fig. 3 X4416

*How to read the number boards on Daylight locomotives was explained in a booklet the railroad handed out in the 1950s. (Kenneth G. Johnsen collection)*

*Trip brochure that was given to passengers on the San Joaquin Daylight and the connecting Sacramento Daylight. (Kenneth G. Johnsen collection)*

*"Daylight" Streamliner Southern Pacific RR*

Even bubblegum cards carried pictures of the popular Daylight locomotives.
(Kenneth G. Johnsen collection)


Builder's photos were produced by Lima for their customers, but today are sought after by collectors. (Kenneth G. Johnsen collection)

## Collectors, Modelers, and Historians' Resources

The striking good looks of the Daylight locomotives captured the fancy of many people, both railfan and daisypicker alike, in the 1940s and 1950s. Much more film was expended on them than on their compatriots. (For example, photos to illustrate this book are plentiful; try writing a book on the Daylights' Central of Georgia brethren and see what you can find!)

Lima Locomotive Works was very good about photographing their products, as was the practice among locomotive builders of the day. Besides detail black and white photos, many of which are still available from Allen County Historical Society in Lima, Ohio, the builder produced various types of colored Daylight builder photos for presentation to clients, potential clients, and the like. These are very collectible today and include the following:

The back sides of builder's cards gave specifications about the locomotives they depicted. (Kenneth G. Johnsen collection)

### LIMA LOCOMOTIVE WORKS, INCORPORATED
#### LIMA, OHIO

Road No. 4436
Order Covers 20 Locos. 4430-4449

Built for SOUTHERN PACIFIC LINES

Class: 484-S-475
R. R. Class: GS-4

| GAUGE OF TRACK | DRIVING WHEEL DIAMETER | FUEL KIND | CYLINDERS | | BOILER | | FIREBOX | |
|---|---|---|---|---|---|---|---|---|
| | | | DIAMETER | STROKE | DIAMETER | PRESSURE | LENGTH | WIDTH |
| | | | 25½" | 32" | 86" O. D. | 300 LBS. | 127⅛" | 102¼" |
| 4'-8½" | 80" | OIL | | | | | | |

| | TRACTIVE POWER | | FACTOR OF ADHESION | TUBES & FLUES | | |
|---|---|---|---|---|---|---|
| | MAIN CYLINDERS | WITH BOOSTER | | NUMBER | DIAMETER | LENGTH |
| WHEEL BASE | | | | 49 | 2¼" | 21'-6" |
| | | | | 198 | 3½" | |
| | 64760 | 77760 | 4.26 | | | |

| DRIVING | ENGINE | ENGINE AND TENDER |
|---|---|---|
| 21'-6" | 47'-8" | 96'-3" |

| | | AVERAGE WEIGHT IN WORKING ORDER, POUNDS | | | | GRATE AREA SQ. FT. | HEATING SURFACES, SQUARE FEET | | | | |
|---|---|---|---|---|---|---|---|---|---|---|---|
| | | TRAILER | | TOTAL ENGINE | TENDER ⅔ LOAD | | TUBES | FLUES | FIREBOX & COMB. CHAM. | TOTAL | SUPER-HEATER |
| ON DRIVERS | TRUCK | FRONT AXLE | REAR AXLE | | | | | | | | |
| 275700 | 81300 | 56000 | 62000 | 475000 | 313730 | 90.4 | 617 | 3885 | 385 | 4887 | 2086 |

Fuel, 5880 Gals.

Tender, Type 12 Wheel

Capacity, Water 23300 Gallons
Equipped with THE LOCOMOTIVE BOOSTER
Negative Order No. 1152

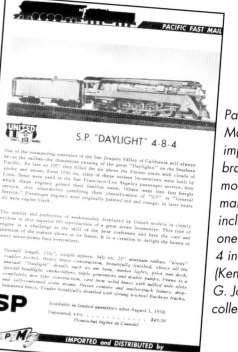

*Pacific Fast Mail has imported brass models for many years, including this one of a GS-4 in 1958. (Kenneth G. Johnsen collection)*

*Daylight locomotives have stirred the hearts of youngsters, including myself, since they were first introduced in 1937. This heavily retouched photo was used to promote toy trains. (Kenneth G. Johnsen collection)*

*Partly because of their enduring good looks and partly because of the 4449, Daylights continue to be a favorite locomotive to model, as is evidenced by this Lionel ad of 2004. (Kenneth G. Johnsen collection)*

Builder Card: A 3-1/4 x 9 inch card with a photo of the locomotive on the front and specification data printed on the back.

Unmounted Print: A 3-1/4 x 9 inch print like the builder card, but without data on the backside and with wording on the front telling the railroad, type, builder, and date.

Lithographed Photograph: 8 x 20 inch, printed on heavy stock. The red and orange parts of the locomotives on these lithographs, as well as on the smaller prints, were blocked out of the photo image and replaced with red and orange ink panels, giving them the appearance of a colored photograph. On Classes GS-3 through GS-5 prints,

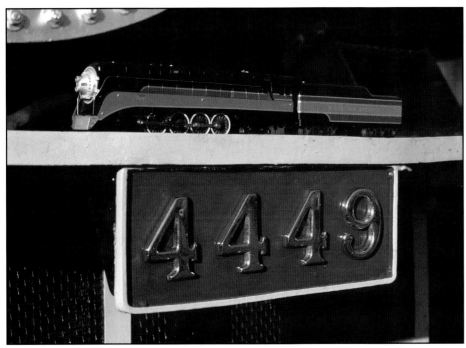

Lionel O Gauge Daylight poses on the pilot platform of the real thing, GS-4 4449 at San Francisco in 1984. (Kenneth G. Johnsen photo)

Tuvalu postage stamp honoring the Daylight. (Kenneth G. Johnsen collection)

Commemorative covers were issued aboard the Louisiana World's Fair Daylight in 1984. (Kenneth G. Johnsen collection)

A 33-cent U.S. stamp honoring the Daylight was part of a 5-stamp set called "All Aboard" issued in 1998. Artist Ted Rose did the paintings. A matching stamped postcard was issued at the same time. (Kenneth G. Johnsen collection)

the silver striping on the locomotive and tender was left white. On the GS-2 print, the silver striping and numerals were added in silver.

Pictures Framed with Glass: The above mentioned 8 x 20 inch lithographs were also produced by Lima and are the most highly collectible of all. Photography was done by Lima's staff photographer of many years, Don Jardine.

Long before the last GS Daylight had its final gasp, Daylight models were available in O scale and HO scale. Over the years since the 1950s, many recreations of the Daylight have been made in N, HO, S, O, and #1 scales. A partial list of manufacturers and importers includes: Con-Cor (N), Max Gray, Westside, Balboa, Lionel, Sunset, Key, Erie Limited, United/PFM (HO), Overland (S), U.S. Hobbies, Precision Scale, Williams, Lionel, Max Gray, Overland (O), and Aster (#1 scale electric and live steam). Even Hallmark has gotten into the act with a Christmas ornament sized Daylight engine and tender.

Stamp collectors have had many cachet covers to collect, as well as a USPS stamp honoring the Daylight. The 33-cent stamp was issued in 1998 and featured a painting by noted rail artist Ted Rose.

Sound recordings of the 4449 abound. But there were a few recordings made of other Daylights in the 1950s when they were still in operation. The classic "Whistles West" was the first 33-rpm record I ever purchased. Produced by the Southern California Chapter of the Railway & Locomotive Historical Society, this collection of

*Ticket to tour the American Freedom Train. (Kenneth G. Johnsen collection)*

steam locomotive recordings included several Daylights.

All of the major videographers have chronicled the Daylight, thanks to the return to service of GS-4 4449, and videos are available for almost every trip the engine has made. In addition to modern-day videos, Daylights have appeared in several films, some of which are available on video or DVD:

*Pal Joey* with Frank Sinatra and Kim Novak. 1957.

*Dear Heart* with Glenn Ford and Geraldine Page. 1964.

*Tough Guys* with Burt Lancaster and Kirk Douglas. 1986.

*Come See the Paradise* with Dennis Quaid and Tamlyn Tomita. 1990.

Most were bit parts, but in *Tough Guys*, the GS-4 4449 played an important role and was "wrecked" in the grand climax of the film, using a full-sized wooden mockup.

Every kid who grew up in the 1950s and had a television set saw the Daylight speed by each week on the

Superman television series, as the caped crusader was being described by the announcer as "more powerful than a locomotive."

The Internet age's great wonder, eBay, has allowed hobbyists to buy models, photos, hardware, books, videos, and souvenirs to enhance their collections of Daylight memorabilia like never before. The American Freedom Train and the 4449's New Orleans trip have produced a bevy of Daylight souvenirs for the collector. Daylight is becoming a household word and a recognizable icon.

For those who would like to learn more about some facet of the Daylight story, allow me to present the following bibliography, which includes many useful resources consulted in the preparation of this book.

# BIBLIOGRAPHY

Ainsworth, Jeff. *Southern Pacific GS Class 4-8-4 Pictorial, Volumes 4 and 30.* Monte Vista Publishing, 1998 and 2005.

Beebe, Lucius. *The Central Pacific and the Southern Pacific Railroads.* Howell-North Books, 1963.

Bergman, John F. *The History of Reedley's Railroads.* Reedley Historical Society, 2000.

Best, Gerald M. and David L. Joslyn. *Locomotives of the Southern Pacific Company.* Bulletin 94, Railway, and Locomotive Historical Society, 1956.

Brueckman, Henry and Jeffrey Moreau. *4449 – The Queen of Steam.* Carbarn Press, 1983.

Church, Robert J. *Southern Pacific Daylight Locomotives.* Signature Press, 2004.

Church, Robert J. *Those Daylight 4-8-4s.* Kratville Publications, 1966.

Cook, Richard J. *Super Power Steam Locomotives.* Golden West Books, 1966.

Diebert, Timothy S. and Joseph A. Strapac. *Southern Pacific Company Steam Locomotive Compendium.* Shade Tree Books, 1987.

Demoro, Harre W. *Southern Pacific Bay Area Steam.* Chatham Publishing Company, 1979.

Duke, Donald. *Southern Pacific Steam Locomotives.* Pacific Railway Journal, 1962.

Dunscomb, Guy L. *A Century of Southern Pacific Steam Locomotives.* Guy L. Dunscomb, 1963.

Hirsimaki, Eric. *Lima the History.* Hundman Publishing, Inc., 1986.

Huxtable, Nils. *Daylight Reflections.* Steamscenes, 1987.

Johnsen, Kenneth G. *Daylight: 4449's Family Album.* Kenneth G. Johnsen, 1984.

Johnsen, Kenneth G. *Pacific: 2472's Family Album.* Interurban Press, 1990.

Menke, Arnold. *The Compendium Companion.* Arnold Menke, 1995.

Ryan, Dennis and Joseph Shine. *Southern Pacific Passenger Trains, Volume 1 Night Trains of the Coast Route.* Four Ways West Publications, 1986.

Ryan, Dennis and Joseph Shine. *Southern Pacific Passenger Trains, Volume 2 Day Trains of the Coast Route.* Four Ways West Publications, 2000.

Signor, John R. *Southern Pacific's Coast Line.* Signature Press, 1994.

Thompson, Anthony W. and John R. Signor. *Southern Pacific's Coast Line Pictorial.* Signature Press, 2000.

Wright, Richard K. *America's Bicentennial Queen Engine 4449.* Wright Enterprises, 1975.

Wright, Richard K. *Southern Pacific Daylight Train 98-99, Volume 1.* Whistlestop Publications, 1970.

Zucker, Joseph. *All Aboard America.* American Freedom Train Foundation, 1976.